EFFECTIVE EMAIL:

Concise, Clear Writing to Advance Your Business Needs

by Natasha Terk

**A self-paced course from
The Write It Well Series
on Business Communication**

Corporations, professional associations, and other organizations may be eligible for special discounts on bulk quantities of Write It Well books and training courses. For more information, call (510) 868-3322 or email us at info@writeitwell.com.

Publisher: Write It Well
PO Box 13098
Oakland, CA 94661

(510) 868-3322

www.writeitwell.com

Previous edition:

Some content is adapted from Janis Fisher Chan's *Email: A Write It Well Guide*, 2nd ed. (Oakland, CA: Write It Well, 2008).

Author: Natasha Terk

Editor: Christopher Disman

To order this book, visit our website, writeitwell.com.

Our publications include the following books, e-books, and e-learning modules from The Write It Well Series on Business Writing:

> *Professional Writing Skills*
> *Reports, Proposals, and Procedures*
> *Land the Job: Writing Effective Resumes and Cover Letters*
> *Develop and Deliver Effective Presentations*
> *Writing Performance Reviews*

Write It Well offers a variety of customized on-site and online training courses, including the following:

> Effective Email
> Professional Writing Skills
> Writing Performance Reviews
> Writing Resumes and Cover Letters
> Technical Writing
> Marketing and Social Media Writing
> Management Communication Skills
> Global Teamwork and Meeting Skills
> Presentation Skills
> Reports, Proposals, and Procedures

Train-the-trainer kits are also available to accompany these courses.

We offer coaching to improve individual professionals' writing and presenting skills. We also offer editorial, layout, and writing services to help individual authors and teams send out well-organized documents in language that's correct, clear, concise, and engaging.

For more information about any of our content or services,

- Visit writeitwell.com
- Email us at info@writeitwell.com
- Or give us a call at (510) 868-3322

CONTENTS

(CONTINUED)

INTRODUCTION

> "Last week, I actually missed an important deadline because a colleague left crucial information out of an email. He gave me lots of information — much more than I needed — and still left out the answer to my question. When it's used incorrectly, even the most efficient form of communication becomes inefficient."
>
> *— Katie Winter,*
> *Senior Manager, PR and Publicity, Mervyn's LLC*

These days, email writing *is* business writing. Email is no longer just a secondary professional activity: a 2010 Plantronics study found that email is now the primary medium for all business communication ("How We Work: Communication Trends of Business Professionals," © Plantronics, Inc., 2010).

As proof of how important email writing has become, Morgan Stanley managers routinely spend time looking "over new hires' emails before they're sent out to clients" (Diana Middleton, "Students Struggle for Words: Business Schools Put More Emphasis on Writing Amid Employer Complaints," *Wall Street Journal* online, March 3, 2011). And the Confederation of British Industry reports that half of British companies "have had to invest in remedial training" for employees' online writing skills (Sean Coughlin, "Spelling Mistakes 'Cost Millions' in Lost Online Sales," BBC News online, July 13, 2011).

While most of us understand that badly written emails can waste time, we forget that they can also create costly misunderstandings, catapult deadlines forward, delay deliverables, lower people's opinion of you, and undermine a career. We've written *Effective Email* to help you and your organization maintain your credibility, project a professional image, and save time for yourself and your readers.

When will they get to the point?

Everyone understands what a headache bad writing can be, but even highly educated professionals write poorly planned, confusing emails. The *Wall Street Journal* reported in 2011 that "Employers and writing coaches say business school graduates tend to ramble" in emails. The global head of recruiting for Morgan Stanley said that the bank's associates "have trouble presenting information in emails to clients. Some tend to write long emails when only a short list is needed."

All of us know the frustration of trying to find the main point of an email buried deep in paragraphs of irrelevant material. You can use this self-paced training manual to prevent your own readers from feeling that same frustration when they read the emails you send out.

What are they trying to say?

It's frustrating enough to struggle through unnecessary text as you try to figure out what the sender wants you to understand or do. But it's even worse to reach the end of your message and still be confused about what the writer's point is. 40 percent of Plantronics respondents "confessed that they have received emails that made no sense whatsoever, no matter how hard or long they squinted at their computer or devices' screens."

This manual will help you clearly identify your own purpose in writing an email. You'll review techniques to use subject lines, opening paragraphs, and closing paragraphs to send crystal-clear signals about why you're asking for someone's time and attention. You'll also be more confident that your writing will help you keep your readers' understanding and respect.

Don't they know I'm drowning in email?

Staying on top of electronic correspondence can feel like a never-ending challenge. Have you ever groaned to see an email that's just one long, intimidating block of text? Busy readers tend to be grateful when formatting techniques give them a road map through a message. This manual shows you how to use lists and headings in emails the same ways you do in longer business documents — helping you send other people the kind of email you prefer to receive.

The beginning and ending of each email can create an important initial and final impression of you as a writer and as a professional. Carefully crafting your subject lines and closing statements can help you get the results you need from each message. You can also use this manual to learn writing techniques to help readers wake up, pay attention to your message, and see you as someone who communicates worthwhile information.

Sloppy writing in an email reflects badly on both the writer and the organization he or she represents. Peter May, president of Greener World Media, tells Write It Well that "It's surprising how many people fail to see that effective language is part of their business skill set and that it's a necessary contribution to their employers' success."

Careless writing can signal a lack of respect for your customers, clients, or colleagues. In contrast, carefully written email stands out. It shows clear thinking and respect for your readers' time — two qualities that can earn you professional respect.

For individual professionals, the ability to write effective email gives you an asset that many employees lack. For managers, investing in email training can boost an entire organization's image. This manual includes tips and techniques you can apply right away to whatever kinds of email you send at work.

How can I get the most out of this book?

Here are a few things to keep in mind as you work your way through this self-paced training manual and its exercises.

USE THIS COURSE HOWEVER IT WORKS BEST FOR YOU. You could use the five lessons as a workbook, taking notes at the end of each lesson to record your own ideas and strengthen your hold on what you've just learned. Or you might use the table of contents to jump straight to the topic you find most interesting or challenging in your own email writing. Review lessons or repeat exercises as necessary.

USE THIS COURSE FOR YOUR OWN PROFESSIONAL DEVELOPMENT. The writing tasks in each lesson will help you communicate more effectively as both a team member and a team leader. See the sidebars on pages 12, 33, and 107 for just a few of the ways you can consciously link your written communication skills with your teamwork, leadership, project management, analytical, and other core professional abilities. See other books in The Write It Well Series on Business Writing for further professional-development suggestions.

CONSIDER USING THIS MANUAL WITH COLLEAGUES OR TO LEAD A GROUP TRAINING. If you're a manager, HR professional, trainer, or team leader, you can purchase the manual for anyone in your organization who writes for work. You can also use the manual as the textbook for a workshop. (See the writing topics at writeitwell.com for information about our workshops' train-the-trainer kits. Or call or email Write It Well for information about how we'd use this manual to deliver an online or onsite workshop for your staff.)

SCHEDULE TIME TO COMPLETE YOUR READING. If you're going through the manual on your own, set aside time to work on it. Turn off your computer, close your office door, reserve a conference room, find a quiet space, or do whatever you need to do to focus on reading and completing the manual's exercises and activities. Give yourself a deadline for completing the course. It's best to complete the entire manual within four weeks since much of the content depends on your remembering concepts from preceding lessons.

APPLY WHAT YOU LEARN TO YOUR OWN WRITING. Before you begin, gather some samples of your past writing. As you complete each lesson, look through your writing for examples of the problematic language you just learned about. Revising your own writing puts your knowledge in practice and helps you retain what you learn. Furthermore, you'll make sure your knowledge is relevant to the particular communication skills you need for your work. The more you practice, the more your writing will project a consistently informed, professional, and credible image.

You're ready to begin Lesson 1: Plan Your Message.

⟳

1   PLAN YOUR MESSAGE

INTRODUCTION

> "Some of the email I get reads like someone's stream of consciousness — as if the writer just dumped whatever was in his or her head onto the computer screen. It would save me a lot of time and trouble if people would stop for a minute and think through what they want to say."
>
> *— Jeff Angell*
> *President, Pura Vida Coffee*

Email is ideal for the kinds of quick messages that most of us send to respond to questions, pass along information, and make requests. We use email because it's quick and easy — more like leaving a phone message than writing a letter. Email may not seem to call for the same kind of planning that a hard-copy memo, letter, or report would.

But email is still writing. Even if you have only a simple message to convey, you'll get better results if you stop and think about why you're writing, identify what information you want to pass along, and decide what you want the recipient to do.

Unplanned messages like the one below waste everyone's valuable time:

> Maggie, you gave me a copy of an article a couple of weeks ago, when we had lunch at Zeke's, you know, that day my car broke down and I had to take the bus so I was late and you almost left? Can't remember exactly what it was, something from the web, all I remember is that it was one of our competitors talking about a new product. Anyway, I told my manager about it and he was really interested, wanted to know what it said and I said I'd look for it, but then I couldn't find it in my briefcase or anywhere. What I was wondering was whether you'd mind sending me a copy. Thanks a lot and I really enjoyed our lunch. Let's do it again soon.
>
> Brad

This message forces Maggie to waste time searching for the main point, and if she's in a rush, she could easily miss why Brad is writing. If Brad had taken a few moments to focus his thoughts, the email would have been much more effective. Here's a more focused revision:

> Maggie,
>
> Would you mind sending me another copy of the article about our competitor's new product that you gave me when we had lunch at Zeke's? I seem to have lost it, and my manager would like to see it.
>
> Thanks a lot. I really enjoyed our lunch. Let's do it again soon.
>
> Brad

The revised message gets the point across more quickly and clearly. All it took was some thought and planning.

Plan your writing

Whether you're writing an email message, letter, project report, or marketing brochure, initial planning is the key to clear writing. Planning means thinking about these four factors:

- Why you're writing

- Who you're writing to

- What you want to say

- What results you need

No matter how pressed you are for time, it's worthwhile to ask these questions for every email you send:

- Is email the appropriate medium for this message?

- Why am I writing this email? What's my purpose?

- Who's my audience? What's my reader's point of view?

- What's the main point? What's the most important message?

- What information should I include? What does my reader need to know?

- What's the best way to organize the information?

Let's look more closely at each of those questions.

Decide if email is the appropriate format

What if you received the three email messages below? Is email the best way to communicate the information? Why or why not?

Dear Daniel,

This is to notify you that you have come in more than half an hour late four days out of the past seven. We spoke about this issue during your last performance evaluation. If you show up late one more time, I will be forced to institute disciplinary proceedings.

Sincerely,

Larissa

•

Hi, Sienna,

Thanks for filling in for me at the meeting yesterday — I owe you one. By the way, I heard that your manager is thinking about leaving the company. His daughter mentioned it to my daughter in gymnastics class. Better keep it to yourself for now, but I thought you'd like to know.

Byron

•

Billie,

I know how you feel about that invoice. I almost lost it and screamed at the finances woman, because she kept telling me she didn't have it. There seems to be some sort of vortex of doom around it because I can't find my copy either, and I know you sent me at least two of them. I feel like shooting myself in the face! I'm afraid to go down to Financial Services myself because at this stage I'd get in a fistfight. There is no reason this should be happening. Could you please send me copies ONE MORE TIME? This will get solved today, or I start building a death-ray laser gun out of office supplies. I would rather quit than deal with this problem anymore! It's become emblematic of my struggles with this organization's bureaucracy and with certain people's incompetence.

Sorry for the tirade,

Parker

You probably agree that email was not the appropriate choice for any of those three messages. Larissa's message to Daniel addressed performance issues, which should always remain confidential and are best addressed face-to-face. Byron passed on a rumor, assuming that Sienna would keep it confidential. And Parker used email to vent his feelings — something he might later regret.

Convenience is not a good-enough reason to use email to communicate sensitive information. For one thing, email is too public — it's more like sending a postcard than a letter sealed into an envelope. It lacks the human interaction that facilitates communication.

Consider the consequences

To make sure email is an appropriate way to communicate confidential or private information, think carefully about the possible consequences of each message. When we address a message to one person, it's easy to think that only that person will see it.

But that's not necessarily true. Email is a public medium, and there's always a chance that people other than your intended recipients will see emails that you send. Before putting your company's secret formula or an employee's medical history into an email, ask yourself what might happen if someone published that information online.

Email is no substitute for a face-to-face conversation or a carefully worded memo or letter that only the recipient is likely to see. It offers none of the human interaction that's vital when your message might upset the other person — for example, when you're criticizing someone's performance. Without the clues you get from facial expressions, body language, or tone of voice, you may not realize that your words were hurtful or offensive.

Also, we sometimes say things in email that we'd never say to someone over the phone or in person. It's all too easy to dump negative feelings into an email and send it off without rereading it or thinking about how the recipient might feel about it.

The casual quality of email makes it easy to forget that it's usually the wrong place for jokes, stories that amuse us, or words or images that poke fun at an individual or a group. Some of the things that seem funny to you might offend other people who happen to see the email. In addition to creating bad feelings, offensive email can get you — and your organization — in a lot of trouble.

What if email containing these remarks ended up in the wrong person's inbox?

> ... and Malcolm is the positively WORST boss I've ever had — he's
> rude and petty, and he knows nothing about this business!

> •

> ... Keep this under your hat, but we're about to be bought out by
> Acme Industries.... It'll be a real shake-up around here but the stock
> should really take off....

Finally, the body of an email is not usually the best way to convey complex information, such as a detailed report. It's hard to read that kind of information on a laptop screen, let alone on a phone. To preserve formatting and make that kind of detailed document more useful for the recipient, send it as an attachment that describes — and perhaps summarizes — the extra file's contents.

ASK YOURSELF—

Think about the emails you've sent and received at work. Try to remember messages that you found entertaining — either because you told a joke or someone sent you a joke. Would it be all right for anyone else to see these emails?

Does thinking of email as a public medium change how you feel about the tone of any particular email that you've sent or received? Does it change what tone you'll aim for in your emails from now on?

How to decide what's appropriate

Here are some planning questions to help you decide whether any content is appropriate for an email:

- Does the formatting need to be preserved for this information — e.g., for a list with two levels of bullet points?

- Does my organization have any rules against this type of email?

- How would I feel if I received this kind of information in an email?

- What could happen if someone else, besides my intended recipient, receives this message?

- Would I actually say these words on the phone or to this person's face?

- Is anyone likely to be offended by the content of this email? Is it possible that this email could become part of a legal action?

Have you ever received an inappropriate email? How did you feel about it? Did other people see it? Were there any consequences? Did it affect the business relationship?

Were any of the messages you sent within the last two weeks not appropriate for email? What would have been a better way to communicate that information — or should it have been communicated at all?

Decide what your purpose is

Read this message quickly. Can you state the writer's purpose in a single sentence?

> To my team,
>
> Thanks so much for all your hard work during the past six months! We would never have exceeded our goals without your efforts, creativity, and enthusiasm. The attached sales report indicates a 10% increase over sales for the same period last year — you can all be proud. We have to address a difficult challenge. Our marketing budget for the next quarter has been cut by 25%. We need to come up with ideas to achieve the same results — or better results — with fewer expenditures. Please come to next week's meeting ready to brainstorm ways we can do that.
>
> Jennifer

It's not clear whether Jennifer wrote that email to tell her team members how pleased she is with their performance or to encourage them to come up with ideas for saving money. She probably wanted to do both. But the two messages end up almost canceling each other out. Too often, we write email out of habit, without thinking about why we're writing.

Email and purpose

Email is often critical in good professional teamwork, and team members and leaders communicate more effectively when they identify their primary purpose for each email. **Team leaders** often need to communicate a clear vision in writing — e.g.,

- To give team members precise information
- To persuade them of the importance of an activity
- Or to pass on clear instructions

Team members also need to have a clear grasp on the purpose of their emails. A team often works more effectively when its members use email to highlight a shared purpose — e.g.,

- By explaining they need further information
- By providing clear, informative progress updates
- Or by persuasively suggesting possible courses of action

You'll find that email is a more effective communication tool when you know exactly what you want to accomplish by sending a message. For example, do you want to do any of the following?

- Answer or ask a question?
- Verify information?
- Send someone a document?
- Promote a good idea?
- Make your opinion known?
- Defend your point of view?
- Justify a request?

Or do you ever send email for these purposes?

- To give advice?
- To convince someone to take action?
- To sell something?
- To ask for help?
- To thank someone or show your appreciation?

ASK YOURSELF—

Another way to frame all the questions above is to ask yourself, "What **business need** does this particular email serve?"

What was the most important work email you sent in the last week? What business need did that email serve? Did you consciously identify that purpose for the email when you wrote it?

Of course, many messages have more than one purpose. But writing is far more clear — and it gets better results — when we focus each message on just one primary purpose. That purpose can take one of two forms: to persuade readers to do something, or to pass on information. Let's look at each of these two purposes separately.

Writing to persuade

You write to persuade when your primary purpose is to ask or convince a reader to do something:

> Please send me your comments on my proposal by Friday.

> Please change the procedures for processing invoices.

> Please give me your approval to hire an assistant.

> Please distribute an agenda at least three days before a meeting.

> Please reschedule our appointment.

Writing to inform

On the other hand, your primary purpose may be simply to give readers information. They may need this information to decide for themselves what action they'll take, or they may only need to stay in the loop:

> The reorganization team made several key decisions last week. I've summarized them below.

> Computers will be down for three hours on Friday.

> If you want to be reimbursed for your expenses, you need to submit original receipts.

> We plan to launch three new products next spring. Please see the attached descriptions for details.

> The Board will select a new CEO at its next meeting. Here's a list of the candidates.

Some careful planning can make a writer's purpose crystal clear. Here's a quick quiz: what's the writer's purpose for each of the following messages?

MESSAGE 1

Hi, everyone,

Please send me your agenda items for the quarterly meeting by Friday. I'll draft an agenda and send it back to you for review on March 14. Thanks for your help.

Tran

MESSAGE 2

Dear Ms. Settles,

Based on the information you gave me when we spoke last week, we estimate that the cost of building your new website will be approximately $7,500 and the job will take about four weeks. I've attached a detailed proposal that includes a working process and a breakdown of the costs. Of course, we'll be glad to answer any questions you might have. We look forward to the opportunity to work with you.

Best wishes,

Arlin Margolin

The purpose of Message 1 is clearly to ask readers for their agenda items. For Message 2, the purpose is to tell the reader the likely cost of a project and say how long the job will take. The purpose should be that easy to identify in every email you write.

ASK YOURSELF—

Which kind of email do you write more often for work—emails that pass on information, or emails that persuade readers to do something?

Ask what your reader's point of view is

Communication is a two-way process. It takes place only when the message you send has been received *and* understood by each individual at the other end. The most common reason for failing to communicate clearly is not stopping to think about the audience — that is, not bothering to look at the message from the reader's point of view.

Thinking about your audience helps you in several ways:

- It's easier to decide what information to include

- You're more likely to use the right tone

- You'll get your point across more quickly

- Your message will be more focused

Considering the reader's point of view begins with these kinds of questions:

- What's your relationship with the reader? Do you know one another, and if so, how well? Are your teammates or colleagues from the same organization? Is your reader your manager, a client, or a prospective client?

- Is your reader expecting this message? Is this the first message on this subject, or is it part of an ongoing exchange?

- How much does the reader already know about this subject? Does the reader have enough background information or technical knowledge to understand what you're about to convey?

- Is the reader likely to use the information to take action? Make a decision? Be informed?

- What's the reader's interest in this subject? What are his or her concerns about the subject? How important is the information to the reader? What issues could the message raise? How is the reader likely to feel about this message? Could any part of the email come as a surprise? Be unwelcome news? Be upsetting? Put the reader in a difficult position?

Plan how you'll write to multiple readers

You may be writing to someone you know well who's already familiar with your subject. In that case, the questions above should be easy to answer. But what if you have several readers, with differing levels of knowledge, distinct needs, and diverging concerns?

When you send the same message to several people or to a large group, ask yourself this key question: are the readers' needs, interests, and concerns similar enough to send them all the same message about this topic? If not, you'll get better results by writing more than one email to meet these differing needs.

For example,

- **Do some people need more background information than others?** You might summarize the main points at the beginning of the email and then put the background information below the message or in an attachment. If you do, be sure to tell readers where to find it.

- **Do some people have less technical knowledge than others?** You might send those readers a plain-English version of the technical information you send to your more technical audience.

- **Is your purpose to inform certain readers and persuade others?** In that case, you might get better results by crafting a different message for each group.

Consider style preferences

When you think about your readers' points of view, also consider their style preferences. For example, your boss might prefer getting information in well-organized bullet points, while one of your clients may strongly prefer complete, grammatically correct sentences.

Decide how you'll write to people you don't know

What if you need to write a first email to someone you've never communicated with before? When you know very little about a reader, ask yourself what you do know about him or her. You can usually make certain kinds of useful assumptions based on such factors as the kind of organization the person works for, the person's job or position, and the person's relationship to you and your organization. Those assumptions will help you target your message so you get better results.

For example, your reader might belong to one of these groups:

- **Customer service representatives.** You can assume that they're interested in what you have to say, want to be helpful (after all, that's their job), know a lot about the subject but little or nothing about your specific question or complaint, and receive hundreds of similar messages every week.

- **A prospective client who has asked for information about your products.** You can assume he or she knows something about your business but needs further details to decide whether the products meets specific business needs.

- **Managers in other areas who have asked for project information.** You can assume that they're interested (since they did ask for the information), probably need a summary of key points rather than every small detail, and may not be as technically knowledgeable about the subject as you are.

Have you ever received an email on a technical subject you knew little or nothing about? What did the writer do that increased or blocked your understanding?

Learn about your audience

When your topic is very important and you don't know the recipients, it can be helpful to learn more about your audience. Talk to people who know your readers, search the web, or make a preliminary telephone call to get the information you need to send a focused message.

What's the most important message in this email?

> Hello, Peter,
>
> Your request for information about last year's payments was passed to me from Josh Feldman, who is my counterpart in the Denver office. I conducted research into our records in an attempt to locate the payments that you said were missing. We are in the process of transitioning to a new payments system, which is the reason that my research took so much time. According to our records, your company was paid a total of $2,585.00 last year for consulting services. $260.00 of that $2,585.00 was on check #182394 which was cut on January 7 and the remainder of $2,325.00 was on check #211367, which our records show was cut on May 6. We show no other payments made by us to you during the course of the year. We do not know why there is a discrepancy between your records and ours. I hope this information is helpful. As you requested, I have asked Violet Meersham to send you a 1099 this week. Let me know if I can be of any further assistance.
>
> Sincerely,
>
> Leslie Karposki

What's the point of that email? It's pretty hard to find. Peter wouldn't have to work so hard if Leslie had gotten right to the point and organized the information differently, as in this revision:

> Hello, Peter,
>
> As you requested, I have asked Violet Meersham to send you a 1099 this week. According to our records, your company was paid a total of $2,585 last year for consulting services. $260 was on check #182394, cut on January 7, and $2,325 was on check #211367, cut on May 6. We show no other payments. I hope this information is helpful. Please let me know if you have more questions.
>
> Sincerely,
>
> Leslie Karposki

Using Reply All and the CC line

You can show consideration by *not* sending people emails that they don't need to read. It's OK to send someone a quick email asking if they should be kept in the loop for a specific topic. Reaching out that way shows you're thinking carefully about your audience and respecting their time.

Reply All isn't appropriate when one or more readers *don't* need you to keep them in the loop. Use the CC line for anyone who needs to stay in the loop but won't need to reply.

Here are some rules of thumb:

- You're always responsible for deciding who goes on the To line
- You're also responsible for moving people to the CC line when possible
- Remember that you shouldn't send people email that they don't need to read

Someone on the CC line can always chime in if they have something to contribute.

Ask yourself how people read email

Think about how you read an email message. Do you sit back with a cup of coffee and ponder every word? Probably not. Instead, you're likely to read only the first few lines before deciding whether the email merits any more of your time. If it does, you'll scan the rest of the message to pick out the important points.

To make sure the most important information gets across quickly and clearly, put your main point — the most important message — at the beginning. Then follow with the facts and ideas that support or expand on the main point, leaving the reader with a complete, coherent message that accomplishes its purpose.

The journalistic triangle

Have you ever noticed that the first paragraphs of many news articles contain the most important information? The rest of the article then provides further details that support, explain, expand on, or illustrate that information.

News editors know that readers often scan only the headline and first part of an article. They also know that the final paragraphs of a piece may be cut out or put on a separate webpages. That's why editors often answer readers' most important question right at the beginning, as shown in the example below.

Keep this triangle in mind when you write. You meet two goals when you put the most important information first: you answer the readers' most important question right away, and you provide readers with a context for details that will follow.

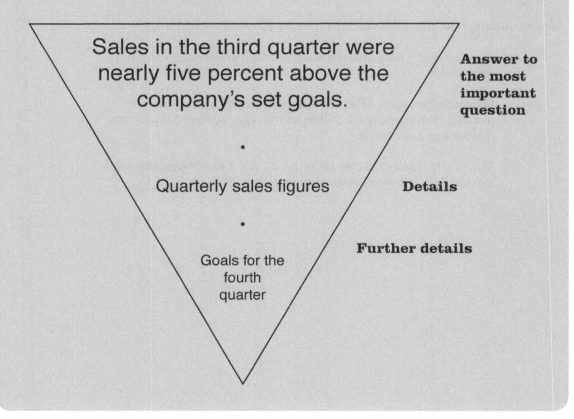

Identify your most important message

Before you can put your main point at the beginning of an email, you need to know what that point is. Try typing out a statement that expresses your main point concisely, in no more than three sentences. Then use that statement to begin your message — maybe adding a few words of introduction to set the context and tone.

Below and on the following pages are some questions that can help you identify your most important message:

Do you need to ask someone a question? What's the question?

> When can I expect to receive the specifications for the new system?
>
> How long will it take to get preliminary cost estimates for the redesign?
>
> Can your team meet with me while I'm in town next Thursday?

Are you sending someone a document? What are you sending and why?

> As you asked, I am sending the report of our investigation as an attachment.
>
> For your information, attached is the preliminary agenda for next month's sales conference. Please let me know by April 6 if you have additions or corrections.
>
> The attached proposal describes details of the health care plan we can provide your employees, including costs.

Clarifying your main point

Here's an easy way to figure out what your main point is: imagine that your reader is in an elevator and that the doors may close any second. You have 10 seconds or less to shout out your message before she disappears into the crowd. What would you say?

Do you want to get approval for an idea or a course of action? What's the key benefit they should grasp?

> Our marketing group has concluded that we could raise our prices by 10% without losing sales.

> The task force recommends that we include a gym in the design of the new site.

> If you agree to add four weeks to the project timetable, we can take advantage of seasonal discounts for workout equipment.

Do you want to make your opinion known?

> I believe we'd be better off postponing the decision about where to relocate until we know more about the county's redevelopment plan.

> After much consideration, it seems to me that it would not be cost effective to reduce staff at this time.

> Your design for the cover of the annual report looks great!

ASK YOURSELF—

How often do you get emails at work that you have to struggle to understand? Do you wish that people who email you would always make the main point easy enough to grasp in 10 seconds? Or in three seconds?

If so, how can you show that same kind of consideration for your own readers' time and attention?

These questions can help you get to your main point right away. Do you want to justify a request? What are you asking for, and why should your reader say yes?

> To meet the deadline stipulated in the contract, we need to hire two temporary programmers immediately.

> Would you be willing to meet me for coffee on Wednesday or Thursday of next week? I'd like to learn more about how you started such a successful business.

> Because we are a nonprofit institution, we'd like you to consider giving us a discount on your e-learning series.

Do you want to give advice? What's the key reason the reader should listen to you?

> I suggest you reconsider leasing the office you told me about yesterday.

> I once had an office on that street, and it was very difficult for my clients to park.

> Because the position requires so much writing, I recommend that you evaluate each candidate's writing skills before making a hiring decision.

> If you still plan to volunteer as Annual Fund cochair, you might want to speak with last year's chairperson to find out how much of your time the job is likely to require.

Think of something you need to communicate by email. Imagine that you have only 10 seconds to get your most important message across. What would it be?

Do you want to sell something? What do you want to sell, and what's the key reason the reader should buy it?

> Our retirement planning advisors can help you ensure that your hard-earned money will be there when you need it. We specialize in working with university faculty like you.

> The next generation of our project planning software has a unique feature that allows team members to be more productive by communicating with each other in real time.

> Our experience facilitating nonprofit mergers can help you avoid many of the problems that result when two organizations join together.

Do you want to thank someone or show appreciation? What are you thanking the person for?

> Thank you for letting me know that our proposal will be reviewed by the end of next week.

> Our team was very impressed with the presentation you gave at our last regional meeting. On behalf of the company, I also want to thank everyone in the accounting department for getting the numbers in ahead of schedule.

Your main point should always come at the beginning of your email. But sometimes you need a few words (never more than a brief sentence or two) to introduce it.

> The deadline we agreed on is coming up fast. When can I expect the project report?

> It was nice to see you at last week's meeting. Your suggestion that we have a fundraising event next April sounds good to me.

Decide what your reader needs to know

> "I'm very tired of reading email messages that go on and on. Why do people think I need to know everything they know? Just give me the information I need, and then stop. Please!"
>
> *— Michelle Black*
> *BCS Learning and Knowledge*
> *IBM Consulting*

How often do you stop and think about exactly what information a reader needs? Most of us do that only for very important messages. As a result, many of our emails include unnecessary information or omit important information — or both.

That's because we tend to focus on the information we want our readers to have, instead of on the information they need. But if you look at what you write from your reader's point of view, you'll see that for an email to be useful, the information it contains should answer all the reader's questions — and only those questions.

It can be tricky to figure out what those questions are. Unless you're writing to answer specific questions a reader has asked, you need to think carefully about what the reader's questions are likely to be.

Here's an example. Suppose Gary wants to recommend that his manager, Margo, hold a brown-bag lunch meeting for team leaders once a month. Margo's question is likely to be, "Why should we hold a monthly brown-bag lunch?" Gary might come up with these answers:

- Keep everyone up to date on projects
- Let people know what's coming
- Share ideas

The main point and the answers to the question create a content outline that makes it easy to write a clear, concise message. Notice that Gary added only a few transitional words and a closing line to the content outline to come up with this email:

> Margo,
>
> I'd like to suggest that we hold a brown-bag lunch meeting for team leaders once a month. That way, we could keep everyone up to date on the status of our projects and let people know what's coming down the pipeline. These meetings would also give us opportunities to share ideas for solving problems. Let me know what you think.
>
> Gary

Responses and acknowledgments

Sometimes you can't respond to email right away. Here's a decision tree to help you streamline your email responses and keep your readers informed.

You get an email. Can you act right away?

YES

NO

Then reply immediately.

1. Acknowledge the request.
2. Say when you'll follow up.
3. Then follow up at that time.

Reading carefully before you respond

When you're responding to an email, read the entire message carefully to make sure that you fully understand the sender's questions and what information the sender needs. If there are several messages in an email thread (a conversation with several replies), then read all the messages. Otherwise, you might respond to only one question when several have been asked.

Writing to persuade: why should readers do something?

In the example above, Gary wanted to persuade Margo to do something. Her primary question would be "Why should I hold monthly brown-bag meetings?" When you write primarily to persuade readers to do something, the content you'll include comes from the answers to that one question, "Why should we/I do it?"

- Why should we hire your firm to design our website?

- Why should I approve your budget request?

- Why should the customer service team attend communication skills training?

The answers to the question "Why" give you the content for your email. Here's another example of a content outline for an email to persuade the reader:

Main point

I believe we should postpone the decision about where to relocate until we know more about the county's redevelopment plan.

Question

Why should we postpone the decision?

Answers

The new area in west part of county may be rezoned.

The county may offer incentives for building in redevelopment area.

Here's the email that resulted from that content outline. Once again, notice that the writer added only a few words — an opening, some transitions, and a closing — to expand the outline into a clear, concise message.

Dear Lisa,

After much consideration, I believe we should postpone the decision about where to relocate until we know more about the county's redevelopment plan.

One of the three plans under consideration includes rezoning an area in the west part of the county. That plan includes incentives for building in the redevelopment area.

You can see the text of the proposed plans at the link below. Please let me know if you need any more information.

Sincerely,

Adam

Writing to inform: what do readers need to know?

When you're writing to inform, your readers may have more than one question about your email subject.

Here's an example. Suppose that Sarah wants to tell a prospective consultant, Jeremy, that her team is seriously considering his firm for a project. Sarah's main point is that her management team was impressed with Jeremy's presentation and his firm is one of three finalists for the XYZ project.

To decide what content to include in this message, Sarah thinks about what questions Jeremy is likely to have. She comes up with this list of questions as a strategy for grouping her ideas:

- What information in our presentation was of most use to you?

- Is there any other information you need from us?

- When can we expect your decision?

Here are the answers Sarah comes up with to complete her content outline. She groups her ideas around the questions she's formulated:

- **Question:** What information in our presentation was of most use to you?
  Answer: Your experience with projects like ours and the ways you handled problems

- **Question:** Is there any other information you need from us?
  Answer: Bios of proposed subcontractors

- **Question:** When can we expect your decision?
  Answer: Within 2 weeks

Sarah's ready to write her email now that she knows the main point she wants to convey and what information Jeremy is likely to need:

> Dear Jeremy,
>
> Our management team was very impressed with the highly informative — and entertaining — presentation you gave at our regional meeting. I'm pleased to tell you that your firm is one of three finalists for the XYZ project.
>
> The factors that weigh heavily in your favor are your experience with projects like ours and the ways you handled the problems that came up during those projects.
>
> Before we make our final decision, we need one more thing from you: biographical information about your proposed subcontractors. We hope to make a decision within two weeks.
>
> Regards,
>
> Sarah

Did the people who wrote the last few emails you received answer all your important questions? Did they include any information that you didn't really need?

Decide how to organize your information

In a well-written email, there's a logical order to the information you present. The main point is at the beginning, and all the other points relate clearly to that main point. Readers should never have to skip around to figure out what you're trying to say.

If you've given some thought to your purpose, your audience, your main point, and any questions the reader is likely to have, the most logical order usually reveals itself. But when you have trouble organizing the information, consider the following questions:

- **DID YOU JUMP RIGHT INTO THE WRITING WITHOUT THINKING ABOUT YOUR PURPOSE, AUDIENCE, MAIN POINT, AND THE QUESTIONS YOU'RE TRYING TO ANSWER?** If so, then you're multitasking — trying to organize the information while you're still thinking about what to say. The result could be a confusing email.

- **DID YOU ADD ANY EXTRA INFORMATION?** Even when we've thought carefully about what we want to say, many of us tend to put everything but the kitchen sink in our messages — as if everything we have to say will be useful for our readers. Stick to the point: all the information in the body of the email should support, explain, or expand on the most important message. If any detail doesn't do that, then either leave it out or use it as the basis of a new email.

- **HAVE YOU SHIFTED DIRECTION MIDSTREAM?** Sometimes we start out writing to ask someone to do something, and suddenly we skip to an entirely different topic. Shifting direction in the middle will confuse your reader. Consider sending two shorter emails instead.

- **ARE YOU TRYING TO PRESENT TOO MUCH INFORMATION?** If what you're writing is too complex, you might use your word processing program to write a separate document and send it as an attachment, using an email as a cover letter.

- **DO YOU HAVE SEVERAL UNRELATED MESSAGES TO CONVEY, OR ARE YOU WRITING TO MULTIPLE READERS WITH DIFFERENT NEEDS?** The result could be a long, rambling message that makes it difficult for any of the readers to find what they need. Think about whether it would be better to write several shorter messages — each focused on one topic or main point and directed at one reader or group. If you want or need to send all the information in one message, summarize or list the main points at the beginning and then use headings to help readers quickly find specific details.

Organizing your ideas for project management

Organizing your information is a helpful process for many professional activities — e.g., **project management.** Clear categories of ideas can give you an overview of all the project details you need to track and complete, grouped by deadlines and types of activity.

Grouping your project details into categories can help you manage complexity, stay on schedule, and not lose sight of the forest for the trees. And clear emails between team members and leaders are often vital to keep a project on track.

Write out your message

If you've followed the suggestions in this chapter, writing a clear, concise message will be as easy as pouring a cup of coffee. Just take the following steps:

- **CONSIDER AGAIN WHETHER EMAIL IS REALLY THE BEST WAY TO COMMUNICATE THE INFORMATION,** especially for sensitive, complex, or high-stakes situations. For those situations, use your word processing program to draft the message. That way, you won't risk sending it before you're ready — you can review and edit your language first.

- **USE CLEAR, CONCISE, ACTIVE, SPECIFIC LANGUAGE** that helps get your message across as quickly and accurately as possible. (Lessons 3 and 4 of this course will show you how!)

- **BE SURE TO PUT YOUR MAIN POINT AT THE BEGINNING.** If necessary, include a few words or a brief sentence or two that establishes the context. For example, if you're responding to a question, you might restate or summarize the question before launching into the main point: "You asked how much more it would cost to complete the job a week earlier. Here's our estimate of the cost."

If you find yourself adding a lot of extra information, stop and think the situation through one more time. You may not have adequately considered what information your reader needs.

If you're struggling to find the right words to express yourself, then stop. Take another look at your audience and what you want to say. You may be mixing your messages, or you may not have clarified your purpose. Work out the problem before you continue writing.

Use email templates to save time

"My job requires that I write the same six or eight email messages over and over. There are always minor changes, but the purpose and content are essentially the same. To save myself time, I copied each type of message into a file I call 'form letters.' Now I just select the right message, make the necessary changes, and send it off."

— *Kathy Brown, Sales Representative*
Sheridan Books

Form letters, or templates, can be real time-savers. A template provides the basic wording and structure; you need only modify the content to fit the specific situation.

Here are what some simple templates look like:

> Dear [name],
>
> Thank you for meeting with me to discuss ways in which our [name of product] can increase the efficiency of your [specific operations]. I've attached a price list that includes a standard installation.
>
> As I mentioned, we would be glad to provide detailed costs for customizing our [name of product] to meet your company's specific needs.
>
> Please let me know if you have questions. Otherwise, I'll get in touch with you in two weeks to see what decision you have made.
>
> Regards,
>
> Jocelyn Yamamoto

Here are two more templates.

> Hi Sales Team,
>
> This is a reminder of the monthly meeting: [date, time, and location]. I've attached a preliminary agenda. Please send me any additions or corrections at least four days before the meeting. Also, please let me know if you will be unable to attend.
>
> Thanks,
>
> Brenda

> To the Events Coordinator:
>
> My group is looking for a site to hold a two-day training program on [dates]. If your facility is available on those dates, please provide information on the following: [requirements].
>
> If you have questions, please send me an email or call me at the number below. We would appreciate receiving your response by [date].
>
> Sincerely,
>
> Marietta Brown

Situations like these lend themselves to templates:

- Meeting announcements, agendas, and minutes
- Common requests and responses to common questions
- Regular status reports and project updates
- Sales letters and other marketing messages
- Problem reports
- Trip reports

Guidelines for using templates

Here are four situations to consider as you integrate templates into your email program and work habits.

- **IF YOU'D LIKE TO HAVE A TEMPLATE LIBRARY BUT AREN'T SURE WHERE TO START,** create a template folder in your email program and let it evolve naturally by adding basic messages over time. Add a template any time you become aware that you're sending essentially the same message over and over again.

- **TO STAY UP TO DATE,** revise messages when things change.

- **BEFORE YOU START USING A TEMPLATE FOR A GIVEN EMAIL,** ask yourself whether it's a good fit for the specific business need that's motivating you to write that particular message. Copy and paste paragraphs between templates or recent emails if recycling text would save time.

- **WHEN YOU'RE DONE WRITING YOUR EMAIL,** ask yourself whether you've adapted all the template language to the specific writing needs at hand.

> Do you use templates? How well are they working? If you aren't using templates, how could you use them to streamline your writing process?

Adapt your email for mobile devices

Many professionals read and write email while we're on the move, using mobile devices such as a smartphone instead of a computer. A tablet offers viewing and typing options similar to a laptop's, but email is different on a smaller, handheld mobile device such as a phone. Here are some of the advantages and drawbacks to using handheld devices for email.

ADVANTAGES

Here are some benefits to using handhelds for email:

- It's a quick, easy way to get back to people with answers to questions, suggestions for resolving a problem, or a request
- You can keep messages from building up while you're traveling or on vacation, so there are fewer to deal with when you get back
- You can send a quick email instead of making a phone call, especially when there's inappropriate or annoying background noise

DRAWBACKS

Handhelds pose some response-related challenges:

- Faster responses to messages have raised expectations for a speedy response
- Constant accessibility has raised the expectation of always being free to respond
- There's an increased reliance on email instead of person-to-person communication
- There's more temptation to check email compulsively instead of being "present" and enjoying sights, sounds, and people
- There's a temptation to read and write email in downtime or, dangerously, in traffic

Handhelds also pose some reading and writing challenges:

- It's more difficult to type on a small keyboard
- Your device may suggest and incorporate incorrect spellings or word choices that change your meaning
- Even more email arrives with poor grammar and poor spelling
- It's difficult to read long, complicated messages on a small screen—and messages may be incomplete
- It may be difficult or impossible to view attachments

Tips for using email with handheld devices

Here are some ways to use handheld devices productively for your email:

- **KEEP MESSAGES SHORT.** When you send email that might be read on a handheld device, keep messages short and to the point, and put the key information at the beginning. Limit your messages to one topic. If you need to change topics, then send another message.

- **REDUCE THE NEED FOR LENGTHY RESPONSES.** Try to structure messages so recipients either don't need to respond or can answer in a few words. For example, ask questions that can be answered yes or no. If you need a lengthy response, your recipients may decide to wait until they get to a computer — and then forget to respond.

- **MAKE SURE IT'S IMPORTANT ENOUGH TO SEND AN EMAIL RIGHT AWAY.** If you're away from your computer, consider whether it would be more efficient and effective to make a phone call or wait until you're back at your desk.

- **DESCRIBE ATTACHMENTS.** When you send email to people on the move, always describe attachments, briefly, because they may not be able to see them right away.

- **VISUALIZE YOUR MESSAGE ON A COMPUTER SCREEN.** When you send messages from a handheld device, remember that recipients may read your messages on their computer, and not on another handheld. Ask yourself what your message will look like with a lot of abbreviations, or with nonstandard grammar, punctuation, and spelling.

Finally, remember to turn your device off sometimes. To keep email from engulfing your life, remember to give yourself breaks from online connectedness.

ASK YOURSELF —

Do you use any forms of social media that limit how long your message can be — e.g., 140 or 250 characters? If so, does that space limitation actually help you focus your messages?

Could your work email benefit if you adopted a similar mind set — as if you had a limited budget for space and had to make each word count?

Instant messaging

Instant messaging is electronic communication that happens in real time. If you think of email as an electronic form of a letter or memo that needs to be delivered, you can think of IM as a conversation, like meeting at the water cooler or stopping by someone's office for a chat.

Just as everyone involved in a phone call needs to be on the phone at the same time, everyone involved in an IM conversation needs to be online at the same time. Like email, an IM conversation can be saved and carried out on a computer or mobile device.

IM technology and interfaces can change rapidly. But no matter how sophisticated the technology, it will always be important to keep the following in mind:

- **KEEP IT PROFESSIONAL.** Instant messages tend to be casual — writers often use incomplete sentences, abbreviate words, and use symbols to convey information. That's usually fine as long as the message gets across. But this kind of text messaging language is open to misunderstandings and confusion. The casual IM language you use with your friends may not be appropriate in a business setting.

- **KEEP IT BRIEF.** IM is best for quick back-and-forth exchanges — "Can you take a call at 3 pm?" "Who's coming to the Thursday meeting?" "Did you hear from the client about our proposal?" IM is not appropriate for lengthy explanations or solving problems. Once your messages exceed 10–15 words or you've gone back and forth more than two or three times, consider picking up the phone.

- **SIGN OFF WHEN YOU DON'T WANT TO BE AVAILABLE.** An advantage of IM is that people can quickly see whether or not you're available to chat. Be sure to change your IM status when you aren't available. Otherwise, you're likely to be interrupted or distracted by messages popping up on your screen. Also, when your status shows that you're available, people will expect an immediate response.

- **DON'T CONSIDER IM SECURE.** It can be risky to use IM to communicate with people outside your organization. Just as with email, be careful not to use IM to convey confidential or sensitive information.

Social media lessons for business email

Unfocused writing makes unfair demands on a reader, while concise writing shows respect for a reader's time. Long-winded business emails can feel like a particular chore to read since so much of our email is social and brief.

Twitter gives you a visual warning when you go past 140 characters. Do you ever wish a similar gauge would tell you when your business writing gets too long to hold an average reader's attention?

Professionals can practice eyeballing our sentences for the same kind of concise writing. Try to keep each sentence around 30 words or less. It's best to feel cautious, step back, and rewrite your ideas when you see a sentence get near the 30-word mark.

Here are some more lessons Twitter can hold for professionals:

- Tweeting is great practice for writing sharply focused email subject lines

- Active language helps you stay concise

- Readers like for you to explain your main point right away

- Careful grammar, punctuation, and tone can set your business writing apart on any platform

Customers and clients have limited attention to spare. Keeping your language active, focused, and concise helps persuade them that your messages are worth their time.

APPLY WHAT YOU'VE LEARNED

1. Print out five emails you've received recently, and answer these questions for each one:

    • Was the main point clear, and is it easy to find at the beginning?

    • Was any important information missing?

    • Did the email include any information you didn't need?

2. Print out ten emails you've sent. Do the following for each one:

    • Write the purpose in the margin. Was it primarily to inform, or to persuade? Do you think your purpose was clear to your readers?

    • Find the most important point and underline it. Where does that main point appear — at the beginning, middle, or end? Or is it missing entirely?

    • Consider the subject. Was it appropriate for email? If not, why not?

(CONTINUED)

3. Think of an email you need to write. Develop a content outline for your message by thinking about these factors:

    - **YOUR READERS.** List several points to keep in mind about your readers, based on what you know or the assumptions you can make.

    - **YOUR PURPOSE.** What do you want to achieve? Is your purpose to pass on information the reader needs, or to persuade the reader to do something? What actions do you want the reader to take?

    - **YOUR MAIN POINT.** What's your most important message? What would you say if you had only 10 seconds to get that message across?

    - **THE READER'S MOST LIKELY QUESTIONS.** What question or questions does this email need to answer? List those questions and then answer them.

4. Think of the messages you need to communicate repeatedly with only minor changes — e.g., meeting announcements, sales letters, and answers to common questions:

    - Choose at least two of those messages, and think about the kinds of changes you need to make for different audiences and situations.

    - Develop an email template for each message that will let you quickly insert details to customize the message for specific readers and situations.

    - Create a folder for the templates in your email program so you can find them quickly whenever you need them.

**You're ready now to structure each email by focusing on each part of it:
its subject line, salutation, concluding paragraph, closing, signature, and attachments.**

2   STRUCTURE YOUR MESSAGE

INTRODUCTION

Now you're ready to apply the planning and framing skills you just reviewed. Many professionals' email is poorly planned, confusing, and long winded. Like any other form of business writing, effective, professional email requires thought and attention.

OBJECTIVES

This lesson will help you with the following challenges:

- Conveying a professional image of yourself and your organization by considering your tone
- Using your subject line to explain your topic
- Structuring your email to convey information quickly and get the results you want
- Keeping paragraphs easy to skim
- Avoiding trouble by recognizing what topics and information are and are not appropriate

WHAT YOU NEED:

- An idea for a specific email that you need to write for work
- Sample emails that you've sent and received at work

Use your subject line to frame the entire message

Imagine a news website without headlines. How would you know what stories you wanted to read? A well-written subject line is like the headline for a news article: it draws the reader's attention and tells the reader what the email is about. The subject line gives the reader a reason to open the email. It's also your first and most important opportunity to get your message across.

Notice the difference between the original and revised subject lines in the following examples:

ORIGINAL	Changes
REVISION	Health benefits will change Dec. 1: Please enroll now
ORIGINAL	Planning date?
REVISION	Planning Project: Is meeting on Apr. 2, 6, or 9?

The revised subject lines are compelling. They grab the reader's attention and provide enough information to make the reader want to read and respond to the message.

Here are eight guidelines for crafting effective subject lines.

WORD SUBJECT LINES CAREFULLY. Certain words or phrases can send your message to the spam folder, where your reader will probably never see it. Here are a few examples:

For your eyes only	Opportunity knocks
Profit	Confirmation of order
Look at this!	$$!!!!

Your organization may have a list of words and phrases to avoid; check with the people who provide you with technical support.

By the way, always put something in the subject line. A blank subject line is useless to the recipient and may get your message tagged as spam.

INCLUDE A CALL TO ACTION. Do you need someone to send you a document or give you a call in reply to your email? Then add the words "Please send me …" or "Please call me about …" to your subject line. Then readers will understand right away what business need your email represents and how they can help you.

MAKE SUBJECT LINES DESCRIPTIVE AND ENGAGING. The best subject lines both summarize and introduce the contents of the email: try to use them to pique the reader's interest. Notice how the third subject line below includes a call to action: "apply by" a specific date.

NOT DESCRIPTIVE	Program
DESCRIPTIVE	Flextime program starting in August
MORE DESCRIPTIVE	Flextime program: Apply by Aug. 1

MAKE SUBJECT LINES SPECIFIC. An effective subject line includes enough detail to distinguish it from similar emails. It should tell readers what the email is about and also enable recipients to find the email again by searching for a key word or phrase.

VAGUE	Report
SPECIFIC	Robotix computer upgrade project report

WATCH YOUR EXCLAMATION POINTS. In a misguided attempt to call attention to their email messages, some writers try to make the message seem more important than it is.

Only 3 days left to apply!

Your presence required!!

Any subject line with an exclamation point can get your message sent to the spam folder. Furthermore, it's unfair to mislead readers by conveying a false sense of urgency (or humor that may misfire by appearing urgent).

If a message really is urgent, your system may let you flag it or mark it in some way. Better yet, make a phone call to let the recipient know the email is coming and needs immediate attention.

MAKE SUBJECT LINES CONCISE AND CLEAR. A compelling subject line gets the message across without unnecessary words or obscure abbreviations.

WORDY AND CONFUSING

This msg inclds the details abt nu mktg pln

CONCISE AND CLEAR

New marketing plan details

CHANGE YOUR EMAILS' SUBJECT LINES WHEN THE SUBJECT CHANGES IN A REPLY TO AN EAR-LIER EMAIL. In a back-and-forth multireply conversation thread, pay special attention to the subject line. If the focus remains on the original topic, you may not need to change the subject line. But you can mislead or confuse the reader by keeping the original subject line when a reply or series of replies changes the topic of your current email.

CONSIDER THE LENGTH. Long subject lines are often truncated, especially on handheld devices. If you can't avoid a long subject line, make sure the key information appears in its first few words.

> How much attention do you pay to the subject line? Do you usually stop to consider whether it accurately describes and previews the message? Can you think of a time when you changed the subject line when you replied to a message but changed the topic?

TRY IT

Think of a specific email that you need to write for work, and write a concise subject line that meets the guidelines above.

Write the subject line on a separate piece of paper. Then you'll be able to sketch out a structure for the entire email as you read through the rest of this chapter.

Launch your message

Email can save us a lot of time, but it raises concerns that don't come up in the same ways in other business documents:

- How do I make sure my message conveys the right tone?

- How can I format my email to be easy to read?

- Do I always have to use a salutation? A closing? Complete sentences?

These questions don't have quick and easy answers. But the tips and techniques on the following pages will help you send email that achieves your goals and meets your readers' needs.

Read for sense

Keep yourself in the recipient's shoes, and read through your email before sending it. Make any necessary changes to the content of the message right away, before worrying about the formatting, subject line, or other components. If there's any unnecessary information, delete it. If you forgot anything essential, add it.

Stop yourself if you find yourself rewriting the message, moving things around, or adding a lot of new information. Remember your purpose, audience, and main point as well as the questions the email needs to answer.

Read for tone

When you read for sense, also check the tone. Is the email too abrupt? Too casual? Too formal? Not friendly enough?

Abrupt:
Get me the revisions by Thursday.

Polite:
Please be sure to get me the revisions by Thursday.

Polite:
I would appreciate your getting me the revisions by Thursday.

Casual:
Got a lot on my plate right now — not sure I can take on a new gig.

Professional:
I'm very busy at the moment, and I'm not sure I can take on a new project.

Formal:
Prior to July 23, payments can be sent only through the Postal Service. Subsequent to that date, payments must be made through our website.

Friendly:
Before July 23, you can make payments only by mail. But after July 23, you can make payments on our website.

Don't use all-capital or all-lowercase letters. They're hard to read and, respectively, they sound either too demanding or too casual.

Here are some further rules of thumb for tone in email:

- Never send emails that are overly personal
- Never send emails you wouldn't want to be forwarded
- Never show impatience or lack of respect for anyone
- Always try to de-escalate conflict:
    - Reread your email in a calm tone of voice
    - Make sure you haven't let yourself sound angry or dismissive
- Don't be too casual
- Try to actively convey that you feel respect and are attentive

TRY IT

Think again about a specific email you need to write for work — the one you wrote a subject line for on p. 46. Now identify what tone will be the best fit for your message.

Make an email easy to read

How easily can you follow this email message?

> Hi, Laura,
>
> The total contribution you've made for this tax year is $7,200. The maximum contribution for the year is $11,000 plus an additional $1,000 if you are age 50 or older. If Craig wishes to contribute the maximum, he can contribute $4,800 for the rest of the year (12,000 minus 7,200 = 4,800).
>
> If he can get the Salary Reduction Agreement form to me by Tuesday we can take advantage of the last three months in this tax year (4,800 divided by 3 = $1,600). Next year's maximum is $12,000 plus an additional $2,000 if age 50 or older. Our tax year begins with the December pay period (the check that's issued on January 1). I hope this information is helpful.
>
> Best wishes,
>
> Pierre

Pierre clearly didn't think about how that message would look on a computer screen or handheld device. Even though the message is well written, it takes effort to understand it.

Notice how much easier the message is to read when it's broken down into short paragraphs, with a blank line between each one:

> Hi, Laura,
>
> The total contribution you've made for this tax year is $7,200. The maximum contribution for the year is $11,000, plus an additional $1,000 if you are age 50 or older.
>
> If Craig wishes to contribute the maximum, he can contribute $4,800 for the rest of the year ($12,000 minus $7,200 = $4,800).
>
> If he can get the Salary Reduction Agreement form to me by Tuesday, we can take advantage of the last three months in this tax year ($4,800 divided by 3 = $1,600).
>
> Next year's maximum is $12,000 plus an additional $2,000 if you are age 50 or older. Our tax year begins with the December pay period (the check that's issued on January 1).
>
> I hope this information is helpful.
>
> Best wishes,
>
> Pierre

If a message is clearly written and presented, the reader should be able to grasp the important information by quickly scanning it.

Keep these points in mind:

- Short sentences and paragraphs are easier to read than long ones
- Lists are easier to read than sentences and paragraphs
- Information is easier to follow when there's space between list items and paragraphs

Can an email be only one sentence long?

Sure it can. One-sentence emails are fine, as long as the sentence communicates a complete thought.

> Mark,
>
> As you asked, I'll make the necessary changes to the project timetable and send you a revised calendar by next Friday.
>
> Deanna

•

> Marketing Team,
>
> We've scheduled the telephone meeting for 10:30 a.m. tomorrow, May 3.
>
> Billy

Set the tone with salutations

Email doesn't always need to follow the same rules as formal business correspondence. But a salutation or greeting is like saying "Hi" or "Hello" when you begin a conversation. It helps you do three things:

- Establish a personal contact
- Assure readers that the email is meant for them when you use their names
- Set a cordial tone

Salutations or greetings can be formal or informal, depending on the situation. If you're writing to a group, sometimes all you need is "Hi" or "Hello," followed by the first line.

Should I include a salutation?

You should usually use a salutation. You can leave it off when you're holding an extended back-and-forth email exchange, and sometimes when you're providing a brief answer to a question. But an email that begins without so much as "Hi" can seem abrupt.

Your company policy may include guidelines for determining which kind of salutation to use. Otherwise, you can use the ones that follow.

Dear Mr. Wolinsky,	Dear Bob,	Hello, Bob,	Hi Bob,
Bob,	Dear clients,	To my clients:	Hi team,
Hi, everyone,	Hello, associates:		

Should I include commas or colons in salutations?

People often omit the comma between the "Hi" or "Hello" and the person's name for informal salutations:

> Hi Bob,

> Hi, Bob,

Either form is okay. Be sure, however, to add a comma *after* the person's name. It's also more clear to add a comma before two or more names ("Hi, Bob and Allison").

You usually need a formal salutation ("Dear …") only for people outside your organization. But there are exceptions. If you're writing to someone senior to you, such as a director or chairman of the board, it may be more appropriate to use "Dear Ms. Moreno" or "Dear Director" instead of "Hi, Allison."

Are you writing to a colleague or friend? Use an informal salutation or greeting, or just begin with the person's name. It's sometimes better to use a formal salutation when you write to someone you've never met, never spoken with on the phone, or never communicated with by email.

When you reply to an email, note the way the person addressed you. If the person used a formal salutation, you should probably use a formal salutation in return. When you write to someone in another country you may also want to use a formal salutation, at least when you first begin to exchange messages. Many people outside the U.S. tend to be more formal in business settings.

A common question is whether to use a colon after a formal salutation, the way you would if you were writing a business letter.

> Dear Mr. O'Connor:

The evolving style is to use a comma instead of a colon.

> Dear Mr. O'Connor,

Unless your organization's style guide addresses this topic, do what feels right to you.

TRY IT

Look back to page 49. Add a salutation for the email you need to write for work, and match the salutation to the tone you decided on earlier for the entire message.

Use concluding paragraphs to indicate what happens next

A strong concluding paragraph achieves the following goals:

- It makes a final personal contact with readers (a crucial factor when you're writing to persuade)
- It wraps up any loose ends
- It tells readers clearly what happens next
- It uses specific language

A concluding paragraph can also do the following:

- It can restate what readers should do
- It can restate what readers should know

Compare these two concluding paragraphs. Which do you prefer?

Paragraph 1   It would be appreciated if this situation could be rectified in a timely manner. Any questions can be addressed to this writer at the address below.

Paragraph 2   Please find the missing file by June 15. If I can help in any way, please call me at (510) 655-6477.

You probably preferred Paragraph 2. The first concluding paragraph is impersonal and vague. The second is specific to the situation and conveys useful information.

Here are examples of the kinds of clichés that sound as if they were produced by a machine rather than by a person.

> Please contact the undersigned regarding time constraints on this policy.

> Your assistance and cooperation will be greatly appreciated.

> Do not hesitate to contact this writer should you require additional information.

Minor changes can transform those concluding paragraphs by making them specific to one piece of writing.

INSTEAD OF …	TRY THIS …
Please contact the above regarding time constraints on this policy.	Please call John Alcotts about this policy's expiration date.
Your assistance and cooperation will be greatly appreciated.	I will be grateful for any help you can give me in tracking down the correct phone number.
Do not hesitate to contact this writer should you require additional information.	If you need a map or specific directions, please let me know.

Worried about whether your message was received?

Sometimes you need to know that someone received your email, but you don't need a full reply. In these cases, add a line requesting a reply at the beginning or end — e.g., "Please let me know that you got this message."

TRY IT

Look back to page 53. Add a concluding paragraph for the email you need to write for work. You're almost finished setting the email's structure.

PRACTICE

Write a concluding paragraph for this message, feeling free to invent details.

> Dear Mr. Hogan:
>
> Thank you for asking about our new Flexible Loan Program. I'm happy to send the attached brochure, which describes the program and includes an application.
>
> We designed this program after many discussions with customers about what types of lending arrangements they wanted. I think you'll find it offers some unique ways of meeting your financial needs.

_____

_____

_____

_____

_____

_____

_____

ANSWERS

Here's one possible concluding paragraph for the message.

Dear Mr. Hogan:

Thank you for asking about our new Flexible Loan Program. I'm happy to send the attached brochure, which describes the program and includes an application.

We designed this program after many discussions with customers about what types of lending arrangements they wanted. I think you'll find it offers some unique ways of meeting your financial needs.

Please let me know if you have questions about this loan program. If I haven't heard from you, I'll call in two weeks to see if you'd like to apply for a loan under this new program.

Smooth the next steps with closings and signatures

A closing is like the period that ends a sentence—it lets the reader know you're done. Closings can show good manners and efficiency: they let readers know they've reached the end of the message. Your signature also tells them how to reach you.

Closings

Like the salutation, the closing can be formal, informal, or casual.

> **FORMAL**
> Sincerely; Regards; Yours truly
>
> **LESS FORMAL**
> Best wishes; Warm regards; Thank you
>
> **CASUAL**
> Thanks; Talk soon

Choose a salutation and a closing that complement each other. For brief messages to friends and colleagues, it's generally fine to close with only your name or initials. But keep in mind that this kind of closing can have an abrupt tone:

> Parker,
>
> UPS picked up the package today. It should arrive by next Tuesday.
>
> Sheila

•

> Thanks for the update; will let you know if I need more details.
>
> J

Signatures

An email without a signature is like a voicemail without a name or phone number: the assumption is that the other person knows you and knows how to reach you. But just as someone may not recognize your voice or have your number handy, an email recipient may not recognize your email address or know your number.

To avoid these problems, always include your name and number. Repeating your email address in the signature can make it easier for people to find you if they're not replying immediately. And if you use more than one email address, make sure that the email address on the From line is the one you want people to use for a reply.

Depending on the situation and your organization's policy, also include all or some of these details:

- Your title or position
- Your company name
- Your office and cell numbers
- A mailing address
- Your website address

Verify connections through attachment and confirmation notices

Always tell your readers whenever you attach a file to your email. Otherwise, they might delete, forward, or save the message before noticing the important file they needed.

It takes time to open and read an attachment. Save your readers time by telling them what the attachment is, instead of forcing them to open it just to find out. Also include a statement that clearly explains what you expect the reader to do with the attachment.

When you send attachments, consider your audience. Sometimes only your primary reader needs the attachment — the person named on the To line and not the people on the CC or BCC lines. In that case, you might want to send the others a separate email without the attachment.

Also, if the attachment is long and complex, consider summarizing it briefly in the body of the message.

TRY IT

Look back to page 55. Write out an explanation of any attachments you'll include for the email you need to write for work, and then add a closing. Then your email's structure is set.

Consider building on these exercises in the following chapters on concise, clear, well-formatted language — polishing the language you use to fill in a message you can then send to a client, customer, or colleague.

APPLY WHAT YOU'VE LEARNED

1. Check the salutations of ten recent emails you've sent and received. Are they appropriate to the situation? Too formal? Too casual? Too abrupt? How would you change them? Write three of the original salutations or greetings on the lines below. Then write the changes you'd make, below or on some note paper.

ORIGINAL

_____

_____

_____

REVISION

_____

_____

_____

2. Look at five recent emails you've sent and five you've received. Do they have useful closings and signatures? What changes would have helped?

3. Do you already have a signature file that automatically adds a signature block to your email? Do you have at least one alternative signature? If so, review those files to see whether they need any changes.

If you don't have a signature file, create at least two that would be appropriate for the different kinds of email you send. Decide which signature file should be your default — the one that will be added automatically to every message unless you manually select a different one.

If you don't know how to create a signature file, consult your Help menu or the people in your organization who provide technical support.

(CONTINUED)

4. Look through a magazine or some news articles. Circle or jot down some headlines that draw your attention. Notice how the headline gave you a little preview of the article in just a few words. Write out the best three headlines, below or on some note paper.

- _____

_____

_____

- _____

_____

_____

- _____

_____

_____

5. Look at the subject lines from three emails you've sent and three you've received. Do they meet the criteria of a well-written subject line? If not, how could you revise them to be more effective? Below or on some note paper, write in three of the original subject lines and their revisions.

ORIGINAL

_____

REVISION

_____

ORIGINAL

_____

REVISION

_____

ORIGINAL

_____

REVISION

_____

(CONTINUED)

6. Write effective subject lines based on these scenarios:

> Simon needs someone to volunteer to provide administrative assistance for the Heart Association project.

SUBJECT LINE: _____

> Melissa can't attend the Verizon meeting on February 6, but she wants someone to attend in her place and take notes.

SUBJECT LINE: _____

> Grisha believes that the draft of the Clorox presentation needs a lot more work.

SUBJECT LINE: _____

7. Do you regularly send email messages to groups of recipients? If so, review the distribution list for at least one group. Add or remove addresses to make sure that the right people — and only the right people — receive your messages.

Next, you'll learn techniques to keep your email concise.

3   USE CONCISE LANGUAGE

INTRODUCTION

Unnecessary words are obstacles to good business writing. They clutter up your sentences and slow your readers down, and they can also make your email boring. By eliminating unnecessary words, you can keep your readers' interest and make your writing easier to follow.

OBJECTIVES

In this lesson, you'll learn to write more professionally and effectively with these strategies:

- Finding single words for one-word ideas
- Avoiding repetition
- Eliminating wasteful verbs and clauses

WHAT YOU NEED:

- Sample emails that you've sent at work

Here are a few examples of sentences with clutter — words that take up space without adding meaning. Which words do you think are unnecessary?

- Please let me know as to whether you will attend the party.

- The noise level of the trains arriving and departing from the station is low by the current standards of the rapid-transit industry.

- There are several employees who want to take vacations in June.

Here are some words that it would be better to eliminate:

- Please let me know ~~as to~~ whether you will attend the party.
- The noise level of the arriving and departing ∧ *trains* ~~from the station~~ is low by ~~the~~ current standards. ~~of the rapid-transit industry~~.
- ~~There are several~~ ∧ *Several* employees ~~who~~ want to take vacations in June.

In this lesson, you'll practice revising long-winded sentences. Then you'll review your own writing to see if you can make it more concise.

Use one word for a one-word idea

Sometimes you can collapse several words or a long phrase into one word that conveys your message quickly and clearly: for instance, *at a time prior to* simply means *before*. The longer phrase is dull and bulky. The single word does the same job more efficiently.

At other times, you can collapse a multiword phrase into one word by identifying the most important word of the phrase, turning that word into a different part of speech, and cutting out words that don't enhance your meaning.

ORIGINAL	We are in agreement with you about the contract terms.
REVISION	We agree with you about the contract terms.

ORIGINAL	She solved the problem in a clever way.
REVISIONS	She solved the problem cleverly.
	She cleverly solved the problem.

In the first example, the short verb "agree" delivers the full meaning of the longer phrase "are in agreement."

In the second example, "clever" is the most important word in the phrase "in a clever way." The single word "cleverly" delivers the same meaning faster.

Try a practice exercise on the next page.

PRACTICE

Below or on some note paper, eliminate unnecessary words or revise the sentences to make them more concise.

ORIGINAL The client visited the site of the project in May.

REVISION The client visited <u>the project site</u> in May.

1. She drove in a reckless manner.

   _____

   _____

2. We conducted a survey of the members.

   _____

   _____

3. The manager made an offer to buy everyone coffee.

   _____

   _____

4. I believe this procedure will make an improvement in the way that reports are filed.

   _____

   _____

5. He called us in regard to his recent insurance claim.

   _____

   _____

6. Due to the fact that she had been drinking, the accident was her fault.

   _____

   _____

Check your answers on the next page.

ANSWERS

Your answers should look something like this:

1. She drove <u>recklessly</u>.

2. We <u>surveyed</u> the members.

3. The manager <u>offered</u> to buy everyone coffee.

4. I believe this procedure will <u>improve</u> <u>how</u> reports are filed.

5. He called us <u>about</u> his recent insurance claim.

6. <u>Because</u> she had been drinking, the accident was her fault.

Avoid repetition

Business writers often use two or more words that mean exactly the same thing, making sentences unnecessarily wordy. Here are some common repetitive phrases:

alternative choices	important essentials
basic fundamentals	end result
serious crisis	future plans
final outcome	separate entities
past experience	advance warning
surrounding circumstances	two halves
equally as effective as	regular weekly meetings
symptoms indicative of	absolutely complete
desirable benefits	10 a.m. in the morning

These unnecessary words waste your readers' time. A crisis is always serious, plans are always for the future, and 10 a.m. never happens at night!

PRACTICE

Eliminate the unnecessary repetitions in these sentences.

1. The urban residents of the city are unhappy with the new regulations.

    _____

    _____

2. The subterranean garage, located underground, is more secure than the old one.

    _____

    _____

3. Until last week, our group had the best record to date.

    _____

    _____

ANSWERS

Your revisions should look something like these. The underlined words convey the original sentences' full meaning without the unnecessary words you saw on the last page.

1. The <u>urban</u> residents are unhappy with the new regulations.

    — OR —

    The <u>city</u> residents are unhappy with the new regulations.

2. The <u>subterranean</u> garage is more secure than the old one.

3. <u>Until last week</u>, our group had the best record.

Eliminate wasteful possessives, clauses, and *there is* phrases

Some possessive word forms add nothing to a sentence but unnecessary length.

ORIGINAL	Their assumption is that the company should always come first.
REVISION	They assume the company should always come first.

Some sentences can be streamlined by removing unnecessary *who*, *that*, and *which* clauses.

ORIGINAL	The broker who works in Chicago sent the file that is incomplete to the home office.
REVISION	The Chicago broker sent the incomplete file to the home office.

Phrases such as *there is*, *there are*, and *there may be* can also clutter up sentences — either on their own or by requiring extra words after the phrase.

ORIGINAL	There is a new package on your desk.
REVISION	A new package is on your desk.
ORIGINAL	There may be several applicants who have the necessary background for this position.
REVISION	Several applicants may have the necessary background for this position.

PRACTICE

Revise these sentences to make them more concise.

1. The members of the group who are interested in learning more about this software are welcome to attend the demonstration that will be conducted on February 16.

    _____

    _____

    _____

2. Tomorrow's meeting, which will be held as always on the fourth floor, will include a speech about literacy in the workplace.

    _____

    _____

    _____

3. There are thousands of hours wasted because no one can use the files that are out of date.

    _____

    _____

    _____

ANSWERS

Your revisions should be similar to these:

1. **The members of the group who are interested in learning more about this software are welcome to attend the demonstration that will be conducted on February 16.**

   Group members interested in learning more about this software are welcome to attend the February 16 demonstration.

2. **Tomorrow's meeting, which will be held as always on the fourth floor, will include a speech about literacy in the workplace.**

   Tomorrow's fourth-floor meeting will include a speech about workplace literacy.

3. **There are thousands of hours wasted because no one can use the files that are out of date.**

   No one can use the out-of-date files, which wastes thousands of hours.

PRACTICE

Here's a chance to pull together what you've learned so far. These sentences contain several kinds of clutter. Revise them to be more concise and then check your answers on the next page.

1. On the basis of your recent letter, I would like to take this opportunity to inform you that I will investigate the problem about the delay in processing your loan that you mentioned and send you a letter in order to report my findings.

2. At this point in time, it is our understanding that the new computer system will have the capability of processing 50 percent more information than the amount that is processed by our present system.

3. With regard to the current status of your request for additional office equipment, we have submitted a request for the purpose of obtaining the funds that are needed to initiate the purchase.

Your revisions should look something like these:

1. **On the basis of your recent letter, I would like to take this opportunity to inform you that I will investigate the problem about the delay in processing your loan that you mentioned and send you a letter in order to report my findings.**

   I will investigate the delay in processing your loan and write you with my findings.

2. **At this point in time, it is our understanding that the new computer system will have the capability of processing 50 percent more information than the amount that is processed by our present system.**

   We believe the new computer system will be able to process 50 percent more information than our present system can.

4. **With regard to the current status of your request for additional office equipment, we have submitted a request for the purpose of obtaining the funds that are needed to initiate the purchase.**

   We have requested funds to purchase the additional office equipment that you requested.

PRACTICE

Revise the following three paragraphs to be as concise as possible without changing the meaning. Cross out or write in words without recopying the text. Some revisions are on the next page.

During the month of March, the people who are working on the HUF project team made a study of the past history of HUF in order to come to some conclusions as to whether the necessary information was available for the purpose of their determining the project goals.

The people who were members of this study team are of the opinion that the original analysis was done in a hasty manner and there were several errors in the original conclusions. At this point in time, it appears that the main question is a matter of making a decision as to whether you should discontinue the project, or whether the team should undertake and perform a new analysis.

We have enclosed for your information the details that resulted from the study. Due to the fact that the short amount of time is a factor in this situation, we would greatly appreciate your reviewing the information, and your reaching a decision and informing us of it, in a prompt way.

ANSWERS

Your revisions should look something like this.

> In March, the HUF project team studied HUF's history to decide whether they had enough information to determine the project goals.
>
> The study team members believe that the original analysis was hasty and that the conclusions included several errors. It now appears that the main question is whether you should discontinue the project or whether the team should perform a new analysis.
>
> We have enclosed the study results. Since time is short, we would greatly appreciate your reviewing the information promptly and telling us what you decide.

APPLY WHAT YOU'VE LEARNED

Read one or more of your writing samples. If you find any sentences that look cluttered, select two or three and write them below. Then revise the sentences to be more concise.

ORIGINAL

_____

_____

_____

_____

REVISION

_____

_____

_____

_____

ORIGINAL

_____

_____

_____

_____

REVISION

_____

_____

_____

_____

ORIGINAL

_____

_____

_____

_____

REVISION

_____

_____

_____

_____

Next, you'll learn techniques to write clearly in each email.

4   USE CLEAR LANGUAGE

INTRODUCTION

Language should convey your message swiftly and accurately. Some writers try to impress their readers with unnecessarily complex language, which slows down and confuses readers more often than it impresses them.

Unnecessarily complex language can frustrate readers, confuse them, and waste their time. The most effective and impressive writing makes complex ideas seem simple and clear. Simplicity and clarity are qualities that a busy reader will value as he or she plows through accumulated messages in an inbox.

OBJECTIVES

In this lesson, you'll learn to write more professionally and effectively with these techniques:

- Using active language
- Using specific language
- Using plain English
- Avoiding jargon

WHAT YOU NEED:

- Sample emails that you've sent at work

Here's an email written in language so vague, pompous, and passive that it's hard to tell what the writer wants to say.

> Dear Ms. Carelli:
>
> This is in reference to your recent email which has been received and forwarded to the appropriate department.
>
> Please be advised that your complaint will be prioritized immediately and you will be contacted when the nature of the difficulty has been ascertained. Action will then be taken in accordance with the facts.
>
> We regret this unfortunate occurrence. Please do not hesitate to contact this writer if further assistance is required.
>
> Sincerely,
>
> Joyce Ellensby

It's hard to follow, isn't it? Here's what the writer may have meant.

> Dear Ms. Carelli:
>
> Thank you for your email. I am sorry we have misplaced your loan documents, delaying your loan approval.
>
> James Nguyen manages our Research Department; searching for your documents is a high priority for his team. He will send me a report within three days.
>
> I will call you by next Friday with an update on your application's status.
>
> Sincerely,
>
> Joyce Ellensby

The revised email is more concise, even though it includes some new information. The new email also gets the message across more clearly because the writer uses active, specific language, with plain English instead of business jargon.

Use active language

Passive language can weaken your writing, confuse your readers, and make your sentences longer. In contrast, active language focuses your readers' attention and increases the impact of your message.

As you can see in the following examples of active language, the actor comes before the action. To use active language, say *who* acts, and not just what the action is. The actor is underlined in the following revisions, and the action is boldfaced.

PASSIVE	The project was managed by John.
ACTIVE	John managed the project.
	(unnecessary words: "was" and "by") (actor: John) (action: managed)
PASSIVE	The design document has been completed by the team.
ACTIVE	The team has completed the design document.
PASSIVE	A safety plan was prepared and distributed to employees by the committee.
ACTIVE	The committee prepared a safety plan and distributed it to employees.

When you give instructions, it's particularly important to say clearly what you want your readers to do. It can be frustrating and confusing to try to follow instructions in passive language.

PASSIVE   The water should be measured every 35 minutes.

ACTIVE   <u>The technician</u> should measure the water every 35 minutes.

— OR —

Measure the water every 35 minutes.
[an implied <u>you</u>]

These revisions make the passive language active by implying or stating an actor before the action. Either the technician or the reader — "you" — should measure the water.

Sometimes the actor in a sentence is implied rather than spelled out. For instance, in the sentence "Prepare a safety plan," the implied subject is "you." (I.e., "I'm asking or telling you to prepare a safety plan.")

PASSIVE   The cover of the printer should be lifted, the ink cartridges that have been emptied should be removed, and the new ink cartridges should be opened, prepared, and inserted in the appropriate slots.

ACTIVE   [implied <u>you</u>] Lift the printer cover, remove the empty cartridges, open and prepare the new cartridges, and insert them into the appropriate slot.

In this revision, the implied actor — an implied "you," or the reader — now appears before the action of lifting the cover and removing the cartridges.

The next two examples also show how to revise a passive-language sentence by adding a missing subject or actor.

PASSIVE   The door was found unlocked three times during the past month.

ACTIVE   <u>The security guard</u> found the door unlocked three times during the past month.

●

PASSIVE   It would be appreciated if the report could be delivered to me on Monday.

ACTIVE   I would appreciate it if <u>you</u> deliver the report to me on Monday.

The actor in a sentence isn't always a person. Both these sentences feature active language:

ACTIVE   <u>The plan</u> is flawed.

ACTIVE   <u>The weather</u> prevented us from going out.

PRACTICE

Below or on some note paper, revise these sentences so they become active, direct, and clear. The first step is to identify an actor; feel free to invent one.

1. The research project is being conducted by the News Department.

2. A copy of the approval must be stapled to the request before it is forwarded to the Accounting Office.

3. The new design is attached for your review and its return by March 15 would be appreciated.

4. An investigation will be conducted by Andrea Russo into the concern voiced by Mr. Szabo.

5. Reservations for the conference can be made by telephoning Tom Woo at Extension 4732 before December 1.

ANSWERS

Your revisions should look something like the sentences below. The original version appears first, followed by the revision. Make sure that the actor comes before the action in your revisions.

1.   **The research project is being conducted by the News Department.**

      The News Department is conducting the research project.

2.   **A copy of the approval must be stapled to the request before it is forwarded to the Accounting Office.**

      You must staple a copy of the approval to the request before you forward it to the Accounting Office.

3.   **The new design is attached for your review and its return by March 15 would be appreciated.**

      [an implied <u>you</u>] Please review the design and return it by March 15.

4.   **An investigation will be conducted by Andrea Russo into the concern voiced by Mr. Szabo.**

      Mr. Szabo voiced a concern, and Andrea Russo will investigate it.

5.   **Reservations for the conference can be made by telephoning Tom Woo at Extension 4732 before December 1.**

      You can make reservations for the conference by telephoning Tom Woo at Extension 4732 before December 1.

      —OR—

      [implied <u>you</u>] To make reservations for the conference, telephone Tom Woo at Extension 4732 before December 1.

ASSIGNMENT

Do you use too much passive language when you write? Look through sample emails you've written for passive, indirect sentences. If you find any, write two of them below. Then revise the sentences to be active and direct. If you don't find any passive sentences, go on to the next section of this lesson.

If you're not sure whether a sentence is passive or active, underline the actor and circle the action. The language is passive if you can't find an actor (including an implied "you") or if the actor comes after the action.

ORIGINAL

_____

_____

_____

_____

REVISION

_____

_____

_____

_____

ORIGINAL

_____

_____

_____

_____

REVISION

_____

_____

_____

Use specific language

Specific language makes your writing easier to read, while vague language paints an unclear picture. The more specific your language is, the less guesswork and effort your readers will need to understand your message.

VAGUE   Some time ago, the building was destroyed in a disaster.

SPECIFIC   In 1994, fire destroyed the apartment house.

VAGUE   Our group went to Los Angeles for a meeting.

SPECIFIC   Our project team flew to Los Angeles to meet with Harriet Allen, the system designer.

VAGUE   Ask the client to complete the paperwork in a timely manner.

SPECIFIC   Ask the client to complete the new account application form within ten working days.

It can show consideration when you supply your readers with precise information. Vague language can require them to guess at the meanings behind your word choices, so try using words and phrases like the ones listed here to make your writing less vague and more specific.

VAGUE	SPECIFIC
vehicle	car
car	convertible
equipment	computer
computer	laptop; tablet
went	walked; ran; drove
traveled	flew; took the train; sailed
contacted	called; spoke to; visited
proper	print-ready
some	five
recently	yesterday
in a timely manner	by August 15; within two weeks

PRACTICE

Underline the vague, general words and phrases in these sentences. Then use your imagination to fill in details and revise the sentences so they communicate specific, useful information.

1. Recently, we looked at a structure that may be suitable for our needs.

    _____

    _____

    _____

2. During the incident, Ms. Brown sustained multiple injuries to her upper torso and limbs.

    _____

    _____

    _____

3. We have identified a few items to be discussed at the meeting, so please leave considerable time in your schedule.

    _____

    _____

    _____

    _____

ANSWERS

Your revisions should look something like these; the original version appears first, followed by the revision. Your revisions may have very different new details. The original words are vague and imprecise; here are some more concrete terms to replace them.

1:   **Recently, we looked at a structure that may be suitable for our needs.**

Last week we looked at a four-story building that may be big enough for our new machine polishers.

2:   **During the incident, Ms. Brown sustained multiple injuries to her upper torso and limbs.**

During the fall, Ms. Brown's chest, shoulders, and arms were scratched and cut.

3:   **We have identified a few items to be discussed at the meeting, so please leave considerable time in your schedule.**

At the meeting, we will discuss the next conference, the move to the new building, and the new staff position. Please leave at least three hours in your schedule.

ASSIGNMENT

Check your own writing for vague words and phrases. Write two of the phrases you find in the space below and revise them to be more specific and clear.

ORIGINAL

_____

_____

_____

REVISION

_____

_____

_____

ORIGINAL

_____

_____

_____

REVISION

_____

_____

_____

Use plain English

Do you ever have to read something very slowly because the writer used unnecessarily formal or uncommon words when everyday language would have gotten the point across?

Pompous language can confuse, intimidate, amuse, or annoy your readers. Plain English communicates your message more reliably. Stuffy words and phrases can force readers to mentally translate your writing into everyday language, which can waste time and cause misunderstandings.

How long does it take for you to read this paragraph and understand it?

> Per your request, enclosed herewith are documents concerning the above-mentioned project. Please review said documents and return them to this office prior to January 15. We will then initiate the process of implementing the requested system modifications.

See how much easier the paragraph is to read when it's written in plain English?

> As you asked, I am sending a description of the Acme project. Please read the description and send it back to me before January 15. We will then begin the system modifications.

Pompous language gets in the way of your message, so use plain English when you write. Choose ordinary words that communicate your message as simply and directly as possible.

PRACTICE

Sometimes, the words in this list are the best, most precise words to use. But writers often use these words when simpler language would communicate more clearly. What ordinary words or phrases would be good alternatives to the words listed here? Use a thesaurus or dictionary if you're not sure.

1. prior to

2. subsequent to

3. utilize

4. modifications

5. enhance

6. beneficial

7. supplemental

8. magnitude

9. supersede

10. augment

11. heretofore

12. commence

13. endeavor

14. optimal

15. forthwith

ANSWERS

Here are some possible replacement words. You may have different, equally correct answers.

1.	prior to	before
2.	subsequent to	after; following
3.	utilize	use
4.	modifications	changes
5.	enhance	improve
6.	beneficial	helpful
7.	supplemental	extra
8.	magnitude	size
9.	supersede	replace
10.	augment	increase; add to
11.	heretofore	before; until now
12.	commence	begin; start
13.	endeavor	try
14.	optimal	best; most favorable
15.	forthwith	immediately

PRACTICE

Revise these sentences, using plain English and active language.

1. Division managers are hereupon requested to facilitate the implementation of the aforementioned program by forwarding details of their personnel requirements.

    _____

    _____

    _____

    _____

2. The injuries sustained by the passengers during the accident were the result of their failure to use the vehicle's restraining elements.

    _____

    _____

    _____

    _____

3. Enclosed herewith is a heretofore-unseen listing of procedures that must be implemented by our team immediately.

    _____

    _____

    _____

    _____

ANSWERS

Your revisions may look like these.

1.   **Division managers are hereupon requested to facilitate the implementation of the afore-mentioned program by forwarding details of their personnel requirements.**

     Please help us get this program started by letting us know how many people you need to complete the job.

     — OR —

     To help us get this program off the ground, please send us a list of your division's personnel needs.

2.   **The injuries sustained by the passengers during the accident were the result of their failure to use the vehicle's restraining elements.**

     The passengers were injured in the accident because they didn't use seat belts.

3.   **Enclosed herewith is a heretofore-unseen listing of procedures that must be implemented by our team immediately.**

     Here is a list of new procedures that our team must implement immediately.

     — OR —

     Please begin using these procedures at once.

ASSIGNMENT

Look for examples of pompous language in your own writing. Underline any words or phrases you find and write them below. Revise two of them, using plain English.

ORIGINAL

_____

_____

_____

_____

REVISION

_____

_____

_____

_____

ORIGINAL

_____

_____

_____

REVISION

_____

_____

_____

_____

Avoid jargon

Business writing is full of jargon — words, phrases, abbreviations, and acronyms that make sense only to people who are used to business language, or who share a particular job.

Sometimes professionals give new meanings to familiar words, and sometimes they invent new jargon terms. Some of these terms enter mainstream language: bankers' automated teller machines from the 1970s are today's ATMs. *Networking* is another business term that has become widespread and very useful.

However, jargon damages business writing when it's difficult for the reader to understand. You should define any terms that may be new to your reader.

Here are a few examples of business jargon that many reader would find confusing:

buy-in: agreement on what to do

drill down: examine more closely

drink the Kool-Aid: accept without thinking

ducks in a row: elements of a careful plan

leverage (as a verb): take full advantage of an asset or situation

Here are three kinds of jargon you should usually avoid:

Everyday words used in a nonstandard way:

We plan a campaign to <u>migrate</u> customers to our bank.

Words your reader won't find in a current dictionary:

We hope to <u>maximalize</u> our marketing potential.

Potentially unclear acronyms:

Next year's goals include increasing the <u>BOCSF</u>, establishing a <u>RADIT</u>, and improving the <u>FAJ</u>.

See Mallet et al.'s "The Most Annoying, Pretentious and Useless Business Jargon" in the Sources section on page 125 for more tips on jargon.

If you use an acronym, spell out the words the first time you use the term, followed by the acronym in parentheses. Afterward, just use the acronym. For instance, the following sentences could be part of an email to a new intern in an office:

> I'd like you to read the attached request for proposal (RFP).
> Let's discuss the RFP on Monday; after that, I'd like you to start
> writing a response to it.

PRACTICE

Look for examples of jargon in your own writing. If you find any, underline the words and then write them below. Translate two of the jargon words into plain English.

JARGON

_____

TRANSLATION

_____

JARGON

_____

TRANSLATION

_____

APPLY WHAT YOU'VE LEARNED

To apply what you learned in this lesson, revise the following paragraphs so the language is active, specific, and in plain English. Feel free to invent details.

> Enclosed herewith is the information requested by you in your recent communication with the undersigned subsequent to your recent purchase of our computer system. It is our belief that the enhancements described therein would be beneficial to the efficiency of your organization by making it possible to increase the amount of data processed within a given time period.
>
> It is our policy to endeavor to provide the optimum service possible to our customers. Please be advised that should you have additional questions or concerns, every attempt will be made to provide a response in a timely manner.

_____

_____

_____

_____

_____

_____

_____

_____

_____

_____

_____

_____

_____

ANSWERS

Here's one way to revise the paragraphs. The details of your revision will probably differ.

> As you asked, I am sending a description of the improvements we plan to make to the Model 603A computer system you purchased from us last year. We believe these improvements will help your organization process at least 15 percent more data each month.
>
> We try to provide the best possible service to our customers. Please let me know if you have any more questions or concerns, and I will do my best to address them within five working days.

You're ready now to format your email to make it user-friendly.

5   FORMAT YOUR MESSAGE TO BE EASY TO READ

INTRODUCTION

It's easy for email reading to turn into an unappetizing chore. But readers can find your emails effortless to skim through when you use these formatting techniques strategically:

- Use lists and headings to make categories of information easy to grasp
- Use your last paragraph to sum up the email's purpose
- Proofread your message to minimize distractions

OBJECTIVES

In this lesson, you'll learn to write more professionally and effectively with these email techniques:

- Using lists to hand readers your main ideas
- Using headings as signposts for your topics

Use lists to hand readers your main ideas

How do you read business documents? Chances are, you don't linger over the words the way you'd linger over great prose in a novel. Instead, you probably scan the document to pick out the main points and the details you need.

Your goal as a writer is to help readers find information as quickly as possible. To show consideration and speed things up for your reader, look for opportunities to present information in lists.

Read the two examples below. They both present the same information, but the information is much easier to scan when it's in list form.

ORIGINAL

Dear Ms. Fratelli:

To process your loan application, we need the following information and documents as soon as possible.

The purpose of the loan should be entered in Item 3, along with the amount requested. List the balances on your bank accounts in Item 4A. Include the name and address of the institution and the account number. Use Items 4B, 4C, and 4D for certificates of deposit, stocks, etc., as shown.

The name and address of your previous employers should be entered in Item 6C if you have been at your current job for less than two years. Include an explanation of any gap in employment during the past ten years.

In Item 12A, please enter the name and address of the lender who holds your second deed of trust. The current balances on all your credit cards and outstanding loans should be entered in Items 16B and 16C, except for your automobile loans (Item 16D).

Finally, be sure to sign and date the form in Item 23.

The completed form should be sent to the loan processor along with copies of your last two years' tax returns and copies of your most recent pay stubs.

Please let me know if you have questions.

Sincerely,

REVISION

Dear Ms. Fratelli:

To process your loan, we need a completed application as soon as possible. Please send the completed form to the loan processor along with copies of the following two documents:

- Your last two years' tax returns
- Your most recent pay stubs

On the application form, please complete the following items:

- Describe the purpose of the loan and enter the amount requested.
- List the balances on your bank accounts (Item 4A). Enter the name and address of the institution and the account number. List any certificates of deposit, stocks, etc., as shown (4B, 4C, and 4D).
- If you have been at your current job for less than two years, enter the name and address of your previous employers (6C). Include an explanation of any gap in employment during the past ten years.
- Enter the name and address of the lender who holds your second deed of trust (12A).
- List the current balances on all your credit cards (16B), outstanding loans (16C), and automobile loans (16D).
- Sign and date the form (Item 23).

Please let me know if you have questions.

Sincerely,

Leslie Tan

Lists aren't used often enough in email. You can use a list in business writing — and, often, you should use a list — whenever you present three or more related pieces of information. Lists are more effective than long paragraphs in these three ways:

- They communicate information quickly
- They save valuable writing time
- They reduce the chance of grammar and punctuation errors

To make sure your lists are easy to read, follow the five guidelines below. Full illustrations of each of these guidelines follow the list.

1. **Introduce the list.** Every list needs an introductory statement, if only a few words, that identifies the list's theme and puts its items in context. Try to leave blank space between the introductory statement and the first list item.

2. **Make sure that all items belong on the list.** All items on the list should relate directly to the introductory statement's unifying theme.

3. **Be consistent with initial capitalization, sentence structure, and end punctuation:**

   - If you capitalize the first word of one line, capitalize the first word in every line.

   - Items in any single list should all be complete sentences or all be sentence fragments. List items that are sentence fragments should not end in periods, and they do not have to begin with capital letters.

   - For lists of complete sentences, end punctuation (a period or question mark) is only necessary for each item if any one item contains more than one sentence (as this list item does). In any list of complete sentences, you must use end punctuation after *all* the list's items if even *one* list item has end punctuation.

4. **Keep the list parallel in form.** For example, if one item begins with an *-ing* word, then all items should begin with *-ing* words.

5. **Organize the list for your readers.** Lists that include more than five or six items can be hard to follow. Make lists easier to read by organizing the items into main points and subpoints (for instance, as Guideline 3 is subdivided above).

Here are examples to illustrate the five list guidelines you just read.

1. Introduce the list

A list should never stand alone: it needs an introductory statement. The first item in a list can't introduce the list itself.

WITHOUT AN INTRODUCTION

- We offer several thank-you gifts
- A 10% discount on purchases during May
- A discount coupon for the Milano Ristorante
- A complimentary bottle of our best olive oil

WITH AN INTRODUCTION

We offer several thank-you gifts:

- A 10% discount on purchases during May
- A discount coupon for the Milano Ristorante
- A complimentary bottle of our best olive oil

Using lists as a team member or leader

Lists have a wide variety of professional applications, whether you're composing a document as the leader of a company or as a member of a small team — e.g.,

- Setting out a variety of tasks or goals for a strategic plan
- Breaking down intricate processes into tidy, chronological steps
- Breaking down intricate projects into clean phases with specific deadlines
- Identifying which tasks are completed and which tasks remain
- Itemizing a budget and allocating resources for different items

Lists aren't just for word processor documents. Look for ways to include lists in emails, business letters, and short professional documents you write, in addition to longer reports, proposals, and procedures. Whether you're a team leader, vice president, manager, or new hire, list formatting makes it easy for readers to literally follow your ideas.

2. Make sure that all items belong on the list and relate directly to the introductory statement

NOT ALL ITEMS RELATE TO THE INTRODUCTORY STATEMENT

To prepare the room for the training, please do the following:

- Set up the tables in a U shape
- Put two flipcharts in the front of the classroom
- Place the projector on the table in the corner
- <u>Design the training to include lots of exercises and opportunities to practice</u>

ALL ITEMS RELATE TO THE INTRODUCTORY STATEMENT

To prepare the room for the training, please do the following:

- Set up the tables in a U shape
- Put two flipcharts in the front of the classroom
- Place the projector on the table in the corner
- <u>Distribute the printed handouts</u>

3. Be consistent with initial capitalization, sentences or sentence fragments, and end punctuation

Use end punctuation only when at least one item contains more than one complete sentence. In paragraphs, sentences' end punctuation (periods and question marks) tells readers when one sentence stops and another starts.

In lists, end punctuation is only necessary if an item contains more than one sentence. That's because the format of a list clearly shows where one item stops and another begins. It's not wrong to use end punctuation for single sentences in a list. But if you use end punctuation for one item, you must use it for all items.

END PUNCTUATION UNNECESSARY

We are unable to meet the original deadline for the following reasons:

- Two team members resigned in October and we have been unable to replace them
- The client expanded the project scope
- Three weeks of heavy rain made it impossible to complete our investigation

END PUNCTUATION NECESSARY

Here is a summary of our findings:

- The costs of moving to a new location will be higher than we originally estimated.
- According to the most current figures, the total cost will exceed $150,000.
- If we delay the move for five years, we will need an additional 10,000 square feet of space.
- Only 30 percent of our employees say they would be willing to move out of California. <u>Over 60 percent, however, would be willing to consider a move within the northern area of the state.</u>

The following list is hard to read because its format is inconsistent.

INCONSISTENT

We are unable to meet the original deadline for the following reasons:

- Two team members resigned in October. We have been unable to replace them.
- expanded project scope
- Three weeks of heavy rain made it impossible to complete our investigation

The periods in the first item are inconsistent with the complete sentence in the third item, which has no period. The uncapitalized sentence fragment is distracting because its form is inconsistent with the other two items. As a general rule, start list items with capital letters to make it easier to see where each item begins.

Here's the same list in a consistent format.

CONSISTENT

We are unable to meet the original deadline for the following reasons:

- Two team members resigned in October, and we have been unable to re-place them
- The client expanded the project scope
- Three weeks of heavy rain made it impossible to complete our investigation

4. Make sure the items in the list maintain parallel form

The items in a list must be parallel — presented in the same forms. For example, if one item begins with a verb, then all the list items must begin with verbs. If one item is a complete sentence, then all the items must be complete sentences.

NOT PARALLEL

The agenda for the March meeting includes the following:

- <u>Discussion of</u> the new health plan, which will be available to all permanent full-time employees

- <u>Whether</u> to revise the procedures manual

- <u>Early-retirement</u> policy

PARALLEL

At the March meeting, we will do the following:

- <u>Discuss</u> the new health plan, which will be available to all permanent full-time employees

- <u>Decide</u> whether to revise the procedures manual

- <u>Draft</u> an early-retirement policy

5. Organize the list for your reader

As a general rule, keep lists short. There should be no more than five or six items per list. When long lists are necessary, reorganize them as two or more shorter lists under separate introductory statements. (It's fine for a new list theme to be as simple as this: "Here are two further points: • •"). You can also make long lists easier for your readers to scan by organizing the items into main points and subpoints.

TOO MANY ITEMS TO TAKE IN EASILY

Please supply the following for the conference that begins on October 22:

- 30 writing tablets for each meeting room
- Five laptops for the community room
- An overhead projector for each meeting room
- Coffee, tea, and pastry in the foyer each morning
- Four round tables for each meeting room
- A conference phone in the community room
- A basket of fruit for each table in the meeting rooms
- A registration table in the foyer

ITEMS ORGANIZED WITH SUBPOINTS

We will need a number of items for the conference that begins on October 22. Please supply the following in each meeting room:

- 30 writing tablets
- An overhead projector
- Four round tables
- A basket of fruit for each table

Please supply the following in the community room:

- Five laptops
- A conference phone

And please supply the following in the foyer:

- Coffee, tea, and pastry each morning
- A registration table

PRACTICE

Use some note paper or the space below to rewrite this paragraph in list format. Remember to include an introductory statement that tells readers what the list is about and establishes the context.

> The task force found that the customer service representatives need training in how to respond to problems and complaints. There is widespread unhappiness about the quality of food in the cafeteria, indicating the need to find another vendor. How to implement flexible hours without creating logistical problems requires additional study. Finally, field representatives need faster tablets, which have not been included in this year's budget. These are the primary areas of concern the members of the task force believe they need to address during the next six months.

_____

_____

_____

_____

_____

_____

_____

_____

_____

_____

_____

_____

_____

_____

_____

_____

ANSWERS

Here are two ways to revise that paragraph into a list:

REVISION 1

Below are the primary areas of concern the members of the task force believe they need to address during the next six months:

- The customer service representatives need training in how to respond to problems and complaints
- There is widespread unhappiness about the quality of food in the cafeteria, indicating the need to find another vendor
- Additional study is needed to determine how to implement flexible hours without creating logistical problems
- Field representatives need faster tablets, which have not been included in this year's budget

REVISION 2

The task force members believe they must do the following during the next six months:

- Train customer service representatives to respond to problems and complaints
- Search for a new vendor who will improve the quality of food in the cafeteria
- Study ways to implement flexible hours without creating logistical problems
- Find funds to provide field representatives with the faster tablets they need

PRACTICE

Rewrite and reformat this paragraph as a list.

> To help us update our database, please review the enclosed listings
> and notify us of any changes. First, proofread each listing and indi-
> cate any necessary corrections. Then please enter the email address
> clients should use to reach you and at the same time verify that the
> cell and landline numbers and email addresses are correct. Finally, if
> you wish, you may add a maximum of two lines of explanation to each
> listing.

_____

_____

_____

_____

_____

_____

_____

_____

_____

_____

_____

_____

_____

_____

_____

_____

_____

_____

ANSWERS

Here's one way to present the information more effectively. Your version is likely to differ.

> To help us update our database, please review the enclosed listings and notify us of any changes:
>
> - Proofread each listing and indicate any necessary corrections
>
> - Enter the best address for clients to reach you
>
> - Verify that cell and landline numbers and email addresses are correct
>
> - If you wish, add a maximum of two lines of explanation to each listing

PRACTICE

This list has a variety of problems; use the guidelines above to reformat it.

I'm sorry you couldn't join us. It was an important call.

- We discussed a wide variety of topics
- Open the account
- LC documents
- the facility agreement
- Surety bond
- Cash and check deposit and courier services are guarded.
- TPA and product docs
- Please call me with any questions

ANSWERS

Here's one possible revision:

It was important call, and we discussed a variety of topics:

- Account opening

- LC documents

- The facility agreement

- The surety bond

- Guarded cash and check deposit and courier services

- TPA and product docs

Please call if you'd like to hear more about any of these topics.

Use headings as signposts for your topics

Headings have many benefits:

- They make it easier for people to find information. At work, people don't read every word of every document, and people are especially likely to speed-read through emails.

- Headings make email more attractive by creating an organized visual layout. Long, dense paragraphs are a difficult and discouraging way to present information to your readers, while headings are a good way to break up dense text.

- Headings require you to group relevant facts and information together. This formatting makes your document easier for readers to follow.

Headings make your documents easier to understand by presenting your reader with concise themes. Headings are essential if your document is long or complicated or if it contains technical information.

Here's a single email without headings, and then with them.

WITHOUT HEADINGS

Ali:

I hope you can come to the meeting this summer. The annual presidents' circle sales meeting will be held at the Hilton in San Francisco, and you should bring your updated presentations and spreadsheets. You can make travel arrangements yourself or Pam can help you. We'll have one day of learning with workshop leaders including Jamie Hartwell, Linda Lou, and Peter Panino, and one day to look internally at our processes with Jack Deiner.

We're going to Alcatraz. The stay will be three days long with an optional dinner on Tuesday night. Sally is no longer available to help with travel arrangements. Another agenda will be sent out. You can come on Wednesday morning or Tuesday night, but make sure that you're there till Friday morning. Bring comfortable walking shoes. If you make the travel arrangements yourself, use billing code 55789. You don't need to bring anything else. You were selected because you did a great job.

Turn the page to see the email with headings.

WITH HEADINGS

Subject: Annual Presidents' Circle Sales Meeting, July 14–17

Ali:

Because of the great job you did this year, you've been invited to the Presidents' Circle Sales Meeting in San Francisco this summer. Below is all the information you'll need to make your travel arrangements. We'll send you a more detailed agenda by May 1.

Meeting Dates and Location

The meeting will be held in the San Francisco Hilton from Tuesday, July 14th, through Friday, July 17th.

Travel Arrangements

The travel process has changed; Sally is no longer available to help. You can make arrangements yourself using your company credit card and billing code 55789. You can also ask Pam to help.

What to Bring

Please bring your updated spreadsheets and presentations. Also, bring comfortable walking shoes for an outing to Alcatraz on Friday morning. We'll provide everything else you need.

Agenda

- Tuesday: meet for dinner at the hotel restaurant at 7 p.m. (optional)

- Wednesday: meetings 9–5 with Jamie Hartwell, Linda Lou, and Peter Panino, followed by dinner at Aziza

- Thursday: meetings 9–5 with Jack Deiner, followed by dinner at La Mar Cebicheria Peruana

- Friday: morning excursion to Alcatraz; meeting convenes at 1 p.m.

That's it! Please let me know if you have any questions. I'll send out a detailed agenda by May 1st.

Thanks, and congratulations!

Proofread your email

Some people believe that a professional writing style isn't important for email — that the rules of grammar, punctuation, and spelling don't apply. Let's examine that belief. Suppose you received the following message from someone you've never met. What would you think of the person who wrote it?

> Dear Supplier Partner:
>
> I am pleased to announce: that InfoSearch has adcepted a offer, from Online Libary, Inc. to purchase it's website. Marcus Wellenby, Onlines CEO and I have work non-stop in recent weeks to put the deal together with minimum affects for both customers and our supplier partners. This will inable the InfoSearch.com web site to contine to operate and, give it a chance to realize it's potential.
>
> I want to apologize to any of you who have had a difficulty, in contacting us while we have operated with a skeletel staff in anticipation of this transatcion. I also want to personnelly thank you. For your support and for a wonderful asociation to those of you I have the pleasure of meeting.
>
> Best Regrds,
>
> Suzanne Thorpe

Chances are, you wouldn't take Suzanne's message very seriously. It takes a reader more time and effort to decipher careless writing, so Suzanne's writing may seem to suggest she doesn't respect her reader's time. Carefully proofing your emails takes more time, but it also shows that you respect the reader's time.

Careful communication is an important aspect of your business credibility. Remember these key points about communicating through email:

- Email conveys a particular image of you to your readers. If your grammar, punctuation, and spelling are careless, then your image probably will be, too.

- Some kinds of careless writing in emails will mislead your readers or slow them down.

Before you hit Send for any email, do yourself and your readers a favor by proofreading it. The process can go a long way toward promoting a positive, professional image of you and your organization.

Treat email as a vehicle for your professionalism

You probably know from your own inbox that many professionals fail to consider other people's need to save time and stay focused. Formatting your emails so they're easy to skim; sending concise, clear language; and planning your messages are all easy techniques to set yourself apart as a reliable business communicator.

Email is not a trivial medium: all the people we do business with deserve respect for their time and attention. Your readers will appreciate it when you get to the point and stay focused on the business needs that you share with them. The strategic writing techniques you've just mastered will help you project a more credible and professional image with each email you send out.

About Write It Well

Write It Well began in 1979 as Advanced Communication Designs, Inc. We're a firm of trainers and professional-development consultants who help people in business communicate more efficiently and effectively. We offer training, coaching, and writing and editing services.

We provide practical, job-relevant information, techniques, and strategies that readers and training participants can apply right away to the documents they produce and presentations they deliver for their jobs. Many individuals and organizations use our books and training programs — including teams, training specialists, instructors in corporations and businesses of all sizes, nonprofit organizations, government agencies, and colleges and universities.

The Write It Well Series on Business Communication includes the self-paced training courses *Professional Writing Skills*; *Land the Job: Writing Effective Resumes and Cover Letters*; *Reports, Proposals, and Procedures*; *Develop and Deliver Effective Presentations*; and *Writing Performance Reviews*. Visit writeitwell.com for more information about the firm and detailed descriptions of our publications and services.

About the author

Natasha Terk leads Write It Well's business operations and strategy. She holds master's degrees from the University of San Francisco and the University of Manchester, UK. She has served as a program officer at the Packard Foundation, a management consultant with La Piana Consulting, and a board member for the Ronald McDonald House of San Francisco.

Natasha has taught business writing at the University of California, Berkeley and has been a consultant for Berkeley's Haas School of Business. She leads onsite and online webinars and workshops for clients including Dreyer's Grand Ice Cream, Hewlett-Packard, Visa, IKEA, Bank of America, and the City of Palo Alto. She gives keynote speeches and presentations on business communications at seminars and large conferences.

SOURCES

- Coughlin, Sean. "Spelling Mistakes 'Cost Millions' in Lost Online Sales." BBC News online, July 13, 2011. Retrieved April 2013 from http://www.bbc.co.uk/news/education-14130854

- Mallet, Max; Nelson, Brett; and Steiner, Chris. "The Most Annoying, Pretentious and Useless Business Jargon." *Forbes*, January 26, 2012. Retrieved October 2013 from http://www.forbes.com/sites/groupthink/2012/01/26/the-most-annoying-pretentious-and-useless-business-jargon/

- Middleton, Diana. "Students Struggle for Words: Business Schools Put More Emphasis on Writing Amid Employer Complaints." *Wall Street Journal* online, March 3, 2011. Retrieved October 2013 from http://online.wsj.com/article/SB1000142405274870340990457617465178011 0970.html?mod=WSJ_Careers_CareerJournal_2#articleTabs%3Darticle

- Plantronics, Inc. "How We Work: Communication Trends of Business Professionals." © Plantronics., Inc., 2010. Retrieved December 2011 after a download from http://www.plantronics.com/us/howwework/

CPSIA information can be obtained
at www.ICGtesting.com
Printed in the USA
FSOW03n1119241215
14538FS